Purple Hi

Study Guide by Course Hero

CW00847626

What's Inside

👁 Book Basics 1

⊘ In Context 1

🖋 Author Biography 3

👫 Characters 4

📈 Plot Summary 9

🔍 Chapter Summaries 16

❝❞ Quotes 34

🐦 Symbols 37

📑 Themes 38

👁 Book Basics

AUTHOR
Chimamanda Ngozi Adichie

YEAR PUBLISHED
2003

GENRE
Fiction

PERSPECTIVE AND NARRATOR
The novel is written from the first-person point of view, told from the perspective of Kambili.

TENSE
The first three parts of *Purple Hibiscus* are written in the past tense. The final part, "A Different Silence," takes place in the novel's present and is narrated in the present tense.

ABOUT THE TITLE

Flowering purple hibiscus bushes play a symbolic role in the novel, representing both the blossoming that is growing up and a way of living that embraces the new and experimental. The most common hibiscus flowers are red, orange, yellow, and white, but in the novel Aunty Ifeoma has purple hibiscus flowering in her garden. She explains that they are the result of a friend's biological experimentation. When Jaja and Kambili return home, they bring some purple hibiscus from Ifeoma's garden to plant in their own garden—without Papa's knowledge. This act shows that Aunty Ifeoma's progressive attitude has begun to take root in Jaja and Kambili.

⊘ In Context

Postcolonial Literature

Chimamanda Ngozi Adichie's fiction, including *Purple Hibiscus*, is classified as postcolonial literature. The term *postcolonial literature* generally applies to literature produced in certain nations that once were colonies ruled by European countries, such as Britain and Spain. Typically, the term refers to areas of South America, the Caribbean, Africa, and India, where colonialism had a significant influence on the development of the political, cultural, economic, and religious landscape, leading to anti-colonial movements and, typically, independence from the colonial power. Despite the unrest these tensions brought about, colonialism and its aftermath resulted in two or more very different cultures living in the same geographic location and some inevitable amount of blending of these cultures. Postcolonial literature often explores the complex issues of identity and culture through the eyes of characters who exist at the soft boundaries of colonial and indigenous culture. Characters often struggle to find the right balance between these disparate elements as they forge their own identities. A personal identity that is split between two cultural identities, or becomes a hybrid of those identities, is a hallmark of characters in postcolonial fiction.

Nigeria, the setting of *Purple Hibiscus* and Adichie's native country, was a British colony from 1914 to 1960. Nigerian postcolonial literature includes the well-known novel *Things Fall Apart* (1958) by Chinua Achebe (1930–2013), whose work is referenced in the first line of *Purple Hibiscus*: "Things began to fall apart at home when my brother, Jaja, did not go to communion." Author Wole Soyinka (b. 1934), poet Christopher Okigbo (1932–67), and playwright Femi Osofisan (b. 1946) are other prominent Nigerian postcolonial writers.

The means and effects of the colonial project, the anti-colonial reaction, and the blending of cultures in a postcolonial society are all prominent features of *Purple Hibiscus*. Characters represent the broad range of ways that Nigerian people reacted to and adapted to the pressures of colonization. Papa embraces European culture and religion as though it is superior. His sister, Aunty Ifeoma, says he is a product of colonialism. Their father, Papa-Nnukwu, has stuck to traditional Igbo ways and religion. The rift between the two men shows the power of colonialism to divide families and communities. Aunty Ifeoma herself straddles an in-between space in which Westernized ways and Igbo traditions coexist and the tensions between them are tolerated. As a university lecturer and an independent, outspoken woman, Ifeoma also represents a more modern trend in postcolonial literature—feminism.

Nigerian History: Colonization and Independence

Nigeria is home to a number of different ethnic groups, including the Hausa-Fulani, the Yoruba, and the Igbo. In the late 19th century, the British arrived, and the long process of colonizing the country by force began, despite ongoing resistance. Under British rule, European schools teaching Western culture and values spread, as did the use of English and the practice of Christianity, especially in the south. Changes to the economy resulting from new international trade caused migration within the country, as people moved to the cities for work or to agricultural areas to produce crops for export.

The British stayed in power until October 1, 1960, when the country was granted independence. Under the Nigerian

constitution established at that time, the government was led by a prime minister, chosen by election. The constitution also created a ceremonial head of state position. However, tensions between ethnic groups caused continuing problems, which eventually led to a coup in January 1966. During the coup, Prime Minister Balewa (1912–66) was murdered, and a military regime was established under Major General Johnson Aguiyi-Ironsi (1924–66). The coup did little to solve the boiling tensions among the three major ethnic groups, and it was not long before Aguiyi-Ironsi himself was assassinated and another military leader took power. A predominantly Igbo region declared itself the independent Republic of Biafra, and civil war soon followed. The conflict, known as the Biafran Civil War, lasted until January 1970, when the Biafran forces surrendered. Attempts to reconcile the warring groups and return the country to civilian rule were mostly unsuccessful, and coups and assassinations continued.

In February 1976 Lieutenant General Olusegun Obasanjo (b. 1937) became Nigeria's leader. Obasanjo changed the structure of government to include a president, and the first presidential election was held in 1979, placing Shehu Shagari (1925–2018) in the newly created office. Although his administration was known for its corruption, Shagari was reelected in 1983 in an election many considered suspect. Eventually, on December 31, 1983, another coup placed Major General Muhammad Buhari (b. 1942) in charge.

Buhari's administration began as a reaction against the corruption of the Shagari administration and the resulting economic and social decline, and his War Against Indiscipline began. Under Buhari's rule, the government imprisoned many politicians thought to be corrupt. But the crackdown soon spread to journalists and others, causing disillusionment and unrest among the people. In 1985 another coup placed General Ibrahim Babangida (b. 1941) in power. Babangida was likable and gained public support by releasing political prisoners, and at first he allowed more freedom of the press. However, as time went on, he began secretly working against the process of returning Nigeria to civilian rule in efforts to consolidate and maintain his own power. Ultimately, he too was forced to give up his position, and in August 1993 businessman Ernest Shonekan took power, only to be ousted by General Sani Abacha (1943–98) that November. Abacha, though promising once again to work for a civilian government, was a brutal ruler whose administration violently suppressed critics. Abacha was eventually arrested and imprisoned. He died in jail in June 1998 and was replaced by General Abdulsalam Abubakar (b. 1942).

Abubakar was less authoritarian, and his promise to return the country to civilian rule was more sincere. Political prisoners were freed, and critics of the government were given more latitude. In 1999 the country was finally returned to civilian rule under president Olusegun Obasanjo (b. 1937).

Purple Hibiscus is set in the 1980s or 1990s. Although there is no one-to-one correspondence between the story's characters and events to real people and events, certainly events from the time inform the novel. In Section 2 a coup takes place, and Papa sadly notes that coups beget coups in a vicious cycle. He tells his children about the "bloody coups of the sixties, which ended up in civil war." Like many of the coups during these decades, and particularly reminiscent of Abacha's rise to power, the new government begins with promises of peace and then shows itself to be just as violent and corrupt as the previous one. The character of Ade Coker, the journalist killed by a package bomb delivered to his home, is likely based on Dele Giwa (1947–86), cofounder of the Nigerian publication *Newswatch*, who was killed by a package bomb stamped with the Nigerian coat of arms and marked with the words "from the Commander-in-Chief." Nwankiti Ogechi, the prodemocracy activist featured in the novel, is likely based on Ken Saro-Wiwa (1941–95), an activist arrested and executed for treason.

Igbo Culture

The Igbo people are one of the main ethnic groups in Nigeria. Before colonization they lived in small communities, each with its own leadership, though the pressures of colonization and the Biafran Civil War served as unifying forces. Traditionally, villages were made up of compounds, which in turn were made up of several separate households. Each village was typically populated by one *umunna*, or patrilineal group—family relationships through the male line. The wealthy men of the village formed a council that oversaw governance of the village.

Traditional Igbo religion involves worship of a variety of deities, spirits, and ancestors that can influence human affairs and provide protection. Above the other deities is a creator god, Chukwu, with a number of lesser deities below Chukwu in rank, such as an earth goddess, Ala, and the water god Idemili. Shrines honor various deities and spirits, and many contain small wooden figures representing these beings. A personal god or guardian spirit, called *chi*, is given to a person by Chukwu and guides that individual's destiny.

As a result of colonization, many Igbo converted to Christianity, as Christian missionaries set up schools teaching Christian beliefs and customs. There was initial conflict between Christian beliefs and traditional Igbo beliefs. However, over time many Igbo began to practice a combination of Christian and traditional Igbo faiths.

⚲ Author Biography

Nigerian Childhood, American Education

Chimamanda Ngozi Adichie was born on September 15, 1977, into an Igbo family in Enugu, a city in eastern Nigeria that was once the capital of the Republic of Biafra. Two of her grandfathers died in the war of independence that raged in eastern Nigeria from 1967 to 1970. However, several of her relatives survived the war and returned with many stories to tell. The fifth of six children, Adichie grew up in the university town of Nsukka. Both her parents were university professionals who made history at their jobs: her mother was the university's first female registrar, and her father was the first statistics professor in Nigeria. As a child, Adichie was captivated by Igbo writer Chinua Achebe's (1930–2013) acclaimed novel *Things Fall Apart* (1958), which addresses colonial life in Nigeria.

Adichie attended secondary school at the university's school for children of staff, where she was a high-achieving student. After graduating she initially attended the University of Nigeria, where she studied medicine and pharmacy. She left Nigeria for the United States at age 19. At Philadelphia's Drexel University she spent two years studying communication on a scholarship before completing a degree in communication and political science at Eastern Connecticut State University in 2001. She went on to receive a master's degree in creative writing from Johns Hopkins University in Baltimore. From 2005 to 2006 Adichie attended Princeton University as a Hodder Fellow, an honor awarded "to artists and writers of exceptional promise to pursue independent projects at Princeton University." In 2008 she graduated from Yale University with a master's degree in African studies.

Award-Winning Author

Much of Adichie's work examines the postcolonial experience of Nigerians, tackling questions of identity, ethnicity, and power through the lives of vivid, unforgettable characters contending with changing political and economic landscapes. Her play *For Love of Biafra*, published in Nigeria in 1998, is an early examination of the Biafran war. She began writing her first novel, *Purple Hibiscus* (2003), while finishing her bachelor's degree. It won the 2005 Commonwealth Writers' Prize for Best First Book from Africa and Best First Book overall. *Half of a Yellow Sun* (2006), Adichie's second novel, also received several awards, including the Orange Broadband Prize for Fiction. A film adaptation was released in 2013.

Adichie was honored with a $500,000 MacArthur Foundation Fellowship in 2008. The prestigious, highly selective award (also known as the "genius grant") is given to creative individuals from a wide range of fields who are "committed to building a more just, verdant, and peaceful world." The award allowed Adichie to travel more, and she was able to continue her annual creative writing workshops in Nigeria, which she began in 2007.

Americanah and Beyond

Adichie's first post-MacArthur work was *The Thing Around Your Neck* (2009), a compilation of short stories that take place in Africa and the United States. She then spent 2011 to 2012 at Harvard University on a fellowship, working on her third novel, *Americanah* (2013). Unlike her previous works, which are largely about conflict, *Americanah* is a love story that spans two decades and three continents. It is also a meditation on race, cultural standards, aspirations, and assimilation. Widely praised by literary critics and the public alike, *Americanah* received the National Book Critics Circle Award in 2013 and was named one of the year's 10 best books by the *New York Times*.

Americanah was followed by *We Should All Be Feminists* (2014), an essay that originated as a TEDx talk in 2012. Another enormously popular TEDx talk by Adichie is her 2009 "The Danger of a Single Story." *Dear Ijeawele, or A Feminist Manifesto in Fifteen Suggestions* (2017) is a letter-turned-essay originally written for a dear friend's baby daughter.

Adichie currently divides her time between Nigeria, where she teaches writing workshops, and the United States. She is married and has a daughter.

👫 Characters

Kambili

Kambili Achike depicts a life filled with trauma, as her father's violent and cruel punishments for "sin" cause lasting bodily and emotional harm. She is terrified of displeasing Papa, so she works hard at school and sticks closely to the detailed and inflexible schedule Papa creates for her and her brother. She learns to live quietly, ask no questions, and speak in ways that please Papa—or not speak at all. This behavior carries over outside her house as well. Classmates consider her snobbish because she doesn't speak with them, nor does she stay after school to talk and hang out. Rather than snobbishness, however, Kambili's actions result from the lack of conversation at home and lack of familiarity with topics of teenage conversation. Although Papa is abusive, Kambili admires him and is proud of his charitable actions in the community. She has a deep and genuine religious faith that is more than just a product of her father's upbringing. Learning to untangle her personal faith from her father's extreme beliefs is part of her coming-of-age journey. That journey is greatly influenced by Aunty Ifeoma, also a Catholic but more flexible about how that faith is lived out. The lessons she learns at Aunty Ifeoma's prepare her to enter adulthood with confidence, a journey that proves more difficult than anyone imagined.

Jaja

Chukwuka "Jaja" Achike feels protective of both his mother and sister in the face of Papa's violent authoritarianism at home. However, he is also Papa's victim, so there is little he can do to stop the abuse. Like Mama, he quietly attempts to hide things that might make Papa angry. And Jaja tries to keep Papa happy by saying and doing the correct things. He sometimes claims primary responsibility for actions so others in the family will not incur Papa's wrath—until Palm Sunday, that is, when Jaja decides to skip Communion, knowing his father will be furious and inflict punishment at home. What brings Jaja to the point of openly defying his father is his immersion in the family life of Aunty Ifeoma's household. Ifeoma's children openly speak their opinions. They are encouraged to speak out and are not punished for doing so. Ifeoma's blend of traditional Nigerian and Western aspects of their lives helps Jaja see other ways of living righteously—not just Papa's way. Ifeoma's honesty and warmth allow Jaja to confide in her about the abuse at home. These influences lead to a slow and steady opening of his eyes to the value of resisting unjust rulers, even when that ruler is one's own father. Unfortunately, abuse leaves its scars, and though Jaja resists, Papa's violent legacy leads to Jaja's loss of freedom.

Papa

Papa is a devout Catholic with an extremely conservative view of moral behavior. His focus on sin and hell drives his behavior and relationships. Because of his concern that he and his family go to heaven rather than be condemned to hell, Papa violently punishes his family even for thinking about doing something wrong, often weeping as he does so. His abuse leads to permanent disfigurement for Jaja and miscarriages for Mama. Papa also refuses to allow his own father in his home, because Papa-Nnukwu refuses to convert to Catholicism. Papa essentially cuts ties with his father and sister because he believes they may lead his children from the path to heaven. Papa is a study in contradictions. While an abuser in private, Papa is a philanthropist in public. He gives large sums of money to the poor, the church, and family and friends in need. Everywhere he goes, people thank and praise him for his generosity. While privately a tyrant, Papa runs a newspaper that is one of the few willing to be openly critical of the tyrannical government. Ultimately, all Papa's good works in the community cannot outweigh the violence he commits at home. His violent behavior leads to his own violent end.

Mama

Beatrice Achike, or Mama, endures her husband's abuse and watches passively as he violently abuses her children. When Papa beats her, she neither resists nor complains. After each beating she ritually polishes a set of figurines. Although Aunty Ifeoma encourages her to consider leaving the marriage, Mama believes it would be worse for her to leave. Papa is an important man in the community, and she is a Catholic woman.

Thus, she sees divorce as both impractical and immoral. However, when Papa's abuse continues and worsens, it pushes Mama to her breaking point. And rather than leave her husband, she chooses a permanent solution—poison.

Aunty Ifeoma

Aunty Ifeoma is a gregarious woman with a confident stride, a loud laugh, and a Catholic faith that doesn't draw a hard line between traditional Igbo customs and Catholic beliefs. She accepts and encourages debate and disagreement among her children. Though she is not well off, she is hospitable—inviting Kambili and Jaja into her home despite her tight budget and small apartment. Outspoken on matters of politics, she eventually pays the price for speaking the truth when she is let go from her job at the university and must go to America for work. Through Aunty Ifeoma's example, Kambili and Jaja see that Papa's way of raising a family is not the only way and may not be a good way. She shows them it is possible to be Catholic and accept those who are not Catholic. She shows them that speaking up for themselves is not a sin. These lessons are crucial for both Kambili and Jaja as they transition from childhood to adulthood.

Father Amadi

Father Amadi is a young Nigerian priest who is good friends with Aunty Ifeoma and her family. In contrast to Father Benedict, the traditionalist priest at St. Agnes, Father Amadi brings Igbo language, song, and culture into his Catholic faith and practice. He sings along with Igbo praise songs in his car and includes singing in his sermons and prayers. He regularly coaches the youth of Nsukka in soccer and other sports. When Kambili stays with Aunty Ifeoma, she and Father Amadi begin a friendship that moves quickly toward the fringes of romance. However, Catholic priests' vows of celibacy prevent them from engaging in romantic relationships. Although Father Amadi certainly has feelings for Kambili, he cannot act on them. When Father Amadi is reassigned to a new location by the Catholic authorities, he and Kambili bid each other an emotional goodbye.

Papa-Nnukwu

Unlike Papa, Papa-Nnukwu practices traditional Igbo religion, keeps a small shrine on his property, and rises each morning to pray. Because he will not convert, Papa has refused to allow Papa-Nnukwu to come into his home. Furthermore, he restricts Kambili and Jaja's access to Papa-Nnukwu because he believes they will be influenced by his pagan beliefs or will sin by eating or drinking food from which Papa has made an offering to his idol. This lack of family connection grieves Papa-Nnukwu, who believes Papa's stance shows a lack of respect. However, Papa-Nnukwu prays for his son. While Kambili and Jaja are visiting Aunty Ifeoma, Papa-Nnukwu becomes seriously ill. She brings him to her home to care for him, though he dies a few days later.

Character Map

- ● Main Character
- ● Other Major Character
- ● Minor Character

Full Character List

Character	Description
Kambili	Kambili Achike is an earnest, timid 15-year-old being raised in a strict and intolerant Catholic household. Her father, who has high expectations for her, treats her brutally, and she fears his disapproval while craving his approval at the same time.
Jaja	Jaja, Kambili's older brother, is often motivated by his desire to protect his family from punishment. His need to assume responsibility contributes to the novel's bittersweet conclusion.
Papa	Eugene Achike, or Papa, is a strict Catholic who disdains Igbo culture and religion and admires the ways of white people. Although he is an outspoken supporter of democracy, his obsessive preoccupation with sin makes him a cruel, abusive husband and father.
Mama	Mama—Kambili and Jaja's mother—loves her children, but her continued submission to her abusive husband keeps her from intervening when her children are beaten. However, she is the one who poisons her husband.
Aunty Ifeoma	Aunty Ifeoma, a university lecturer, is Papa's liberal-minded sister whose practice of Catholicism embraces a more empathetic understanding of other religions, especially Igbo traditions. She encourages her children to think and to speak their minds, and laughter and conversation fill her home.
Father Amadi	A young, amiable priest in Nsukka, Father Amadi accepts Igbo tradition into his practice of Catholicism. He develops an intense friendship with Kambili.
Papa-Nnukwu	Papa-Nnukwu is Papa's father, who holds to his traditional religion rather than convert to Catholicism. His refusal to convert causes Papa to shun him, regardless of family ties and duty.
Adamu	Adamu is the man who works at the gate of the Achike compound.
Amaka	Aunty Ifeoma's politically savvy teenage daughter, Amaka becomes Kambili's friend and gives her a painting of Papa-Nnukwu.
Anikwenwa	Anikwenwa is an old man who knows Papa and who is thrown off the Achike property for not being Catholic.
Father Benedict	Father Benedict is the parish priest at St. Agnes, the church the Achike family regularly attends. He is white and socially conservative.
Celestine	Celestine becomes the driver for the Achike family after Papa dies.
Chiaku	Chiaku is one of Aunty Ifeoma's friends.
Chima	Chima is Aunty Ifeoma's younger son.
Chinyelu	Chinyelu is a girl who helps out at Papa-Nnukwu's home.
Sister Clara	Sister Clara is a nun who teaches at Kambili's school.
Ade Coker	Ade Coker is the editor of Papa's newspaper, the *Standard*. He is killed by a package bomb after writing articles critical of Nigeria's new government and head of state.
Yewande Coker	Yewande Coker is Ade Coker's wife and, later, widow. After Ade is killed, Papa helps Yewande and her daughter financially.

Ezinne	Kambili's friend at school, Ezinne tries to get Kambili to socialize more so that people will stop thinking she is a snob.
Gabriella	Gabriella is a student at Kambili's school.
Grandfather	Grandfather is Mama's deceased father, whom Papa admired because of his strict Catholic beliefs.
Haruna	Haruna is the man who works at the gate of the Achike family's home in Abba.
Head of state	The Nigerian head of state is the leader of the government after the coup.
Ifediora	Ifediora is Aunty Ifeoma's deceased husband.
The Igwe	The Igwe is a traditional ruler in the town of Abba.
Chinwe Jideze	Chinwe Jideze is a girl in Kambili's class who comes in first in the exams during the first term, beating Kambili for the top scores in school. She thinks Kambili's reserved attitude is evidence of snobbery.
Kevin	Kevin is the driver for the Achike family.
Mother Lucy	Mother Lucy is a nun at Kambili's school.
Mama Joe	Mama Joe runs an establishment that styles hair in Nsukka. She braids Kambili's hair.
Sister Margaret	Sister Margaret is a nun who teaches at Kambili's school.
Dr. Nduoma	Dr. Nduoma comes to Aunty Ifeoma's home to examine Papa-Nnukwu when he becomes ill.
Obiora	Obiora is Aunty Ifeoma's outgoing and realistic son. He wants Ifeoma to be fired from the university so the family can move to America.
Nwankiti Ogechi	Nwankiti Ogechi is an activist who disappears and is murdered. The *Standard* runs a story implicating the Nigerian government in the murder.
Phillipa	Aunty Ifeoma's friend, Phillipa left the university in Nsukka and is teaching in America. Phillipa is the biologist who created the purple hibiscus.
Sisi	Sisi is the Achike family's domestic servant.
The sole administrator	The sole administrator, or head, of the university in Nsukka wants Aunty Ifeoma to stop being so outspoken on political matters.
Chief Umeadi	Chief Umeadi is the only man whose house in Abba is larger than Papa's.

⌁ Plot Summary

Breaking Gods: Palm Sunday

The novel is narrated by 15-year-old Kambili Achike, the sheltered daughter of a successful newspaper owner and entrepreneur, Eugene Achike, also referred to as Papa, an extremely strict Catholic. Kambili lives with her parents and brother, Jaja, in the town of Enugu, Nigeria. The opening section takes place on Palm Sunday. At Mass, Jaja does not go up to take Communion. Papa, who demands academic excellence, total obedience, and Christian piety from his children, simmers with rage for the remainder of the service. At home, his rage erupts. He throws a missal—a book used during Mass—and it breaks a set of ballet dancer figurines on the étagère—display cabinet—that are important to Mama. This day, Kambili says, is when things started to fall apart.

Speaking with Our Spirits: Before Palm Sunday

The novel jumps back in time to explain how events in the family's life lead to the Palm Sunday turning point. Mama, who has been criticized for not giving her husband more than two children, is pregnant. Struggling with nausea one Sunday after Mass, she says she would prefer to stay in the car and rest rather than go into Father Benedict's home for their customary after-Mass visit. Papa becomes angry because she wants to skip the visit with their parish priest, a white, English-speaking man whom Papa greatly admires. Though Mama does get out of the car, in obedience to her husband, and endures the visit, Papa's rage is not satisfied. At home, he beats Mama for even desiring to skip the visit. He carries her out of the door, leaving a trail of blood, which Kambili and Jaja clean up. The next day Mama returns, but she has lost the baby.

Over the next weeks, Kambili struggles to do well in school, though she knows she needs to excel on her exams or Papa will be angry. When she looks at her textbooks, all she sees is blood. She finishes second in her class, disappointing Papa, but he is distracted by outside political events.

At Christmastime Kambili's family travels to Abba, the hometown of Papa's side of the family. There, Papa allows Kambili and Jaja to visit his estranged father, Papa-Nnukwu, even though Papa-Nnukwu has refused to convert to Catholicism and still worships what Papa considers to be a heathen idol in a small shrine in his yard. The children are cautioned not to eat anything while there, not to look at the idol, and not to participate in any pagan rituals. The visit must last only for 15 minutes. Papa himself will not visit, nor does he allow his father into his home. Aunty Ifeoma, Papa's widowed sister, also comes to Abba with her children for the Christmas holiday.

The day after Christmas is a Sunday, and Kambili wakes up having started her period in the night. She has intense cramps and needs to take medicine, but the medicine must be taken with food. Unfortunately, Papa is strict about keeping a fast before Mass, a practice that allows participants to receive the Eucharist. Jaja and Mama encourage Kambili to eat a small amount of cereal, believing Papa will not see. However, they are wrong. Papa comes in, sees her eating, and beats them all.

Before the end of the Christmas break, Jaja and Kambili are

allowed to go to Nsukka to visit Aunty Ifeoma and her children. Aunty Ifeoma's apartment is a sharp contrast to Kambili's home—it is small and shabby, whereas Kambili's house is spacious and luxurious. Ifeoma's home is also louder than Kambili's. Ifeoma encourages her children to debate, laugh, and express themselves. Her home is filled with laughter and conversation, whereas Papa insists on quiet and silent obedience. During this time, both Jaja and Kambili grow in ways that would be impossible for them under Papa's oppressive rule. Kambili develops a crush on Father Amadi, a kind young priest who is friends with Aunty Ifeoma and her children.

While Jaja and Kambili are at Aunty Ifeoma's, Papa-Nnukwu suddenly becomes very ill. Aunty Ifeoma goes to pick him up, brings him to her home, and has him sleep in the room Kambili is sharing with her cousin Amaka. Kambili is terrified Papa will find out she has stayed in a house—and slept in the same room—with Papa-Nnukwu, knowing Papa will believe proximity to the man he calls a heathen is a sin. Papa does learn his father was in the home with his children, and he immediately comes to bring them home. Just before he arrives, however, Papa-Nnukwu is found dead. Back at home Papa punishes Kambili severely for not having informed him of Papa-Nnukwu's presence in Aunty Ifeoma's home. This time, however, instead of beating her he pours boiling water on her feet to remind her that if she walks into sin, her feet will get burned.

Amaka secretly slips Kambili a small painting of Papa-Nnukwu she has created, as Kambili and Jaja are leaving with Papa.

Papa and Ade Coker, an editor at Papa's newspaper, the *Standard*, print a story about a prodemocracy activist—implicating the Nigerian head of state in the activist's death. Shortly afterward, Ade Coker is killed when a package bomb is delivered to his home. Papa generously gives money to his widow and children.

Kambili knows that Papa will be angry if he finds the painting of Papa-Nnukwu, so she hides it in her room. One day she shows it to Jaja. The two of them look at it a little too long, and Papa comes into the room while they still have it out. He flies into a rage, tears the painting to pieces, and throws them on the floor. Weeping, Kambili crumples to the floor on top of the torn pieces. Papa then kicks her until she is unconscious. She wakes up in terrible pain, in the hospital. Papa, Mama, Aunty Ifeoma, and Father Amadi all come to see her in the hospital, and eventually Kambili is well enough to leave. For reasons unclear to Kambili, Papa allows Jaja and Kambili to go to Aunty Ifeoma's home in Nsukka so that Kambili can continue recovering.

Meanwhile, a great deal is happening in Aunty Ifeoma's life. There is tension between her and the sole administrator of the university because Ifeoma is politically outspoken and drawing the ire of the government. Looking for incriminating materials, government agents search Aunty Ifeoma's apartment to pressure her into silence. While all this is going on, Mama unexpectedly arrives, showing signs of another of her husband's beatings. Yet, when Papa arrives to bring them home, they all go with him.

Here, the narrative catches up to the present explored in Breaking Gods: Palm Sunday. The next day is Palm Sunday. Jaja refuses to take Communion. Papa breaks Mama's figurines.

The Pieces of Gods: After Palm Sunday

After Palm Sunday, life changes in the Achike home. Papa seems weak and sick. Jaja is openly resistant to Papa's authority, and everyone seems less afraid. Ifeoma loses her job at the university and calls to tell them she and her family will soon move to the United States. Jaja and Kambili go to Nsukka to have one last visit with Ifeoma and their cousins and go with her on a pilgrimage to Aokpe. On the pilgrimage Kambili senses the presence of the Virgin Mary and sees visions of her everywhere.

Father Amadi is called to a new location to continue his mission work. Before his departure, he and Kambili have an emotional farewell.

Unexpectedly, Papa is discovered at his desk, dead. After an autopsy reveals he was poisoned, Mama admits to Kambili and Jaja that she is the one who poisoned him. When the police come to the house, however, Jaja confesses to the crime to protect Mama. He is arrested.

A Different Silence: The Present

It is three years later, and much has changed. Mama is like a shell of her former self, and Jaja has been imprisoned for a crime he did not commit. Kambili and Mama have gone often to the prison to see Jaja in the intervening years. Now, it seems likely he will be released, as a result of continuing bribes. Despite the violence and suffering her family has been through, Kambili feels a sense of hope.

Plot Diagram

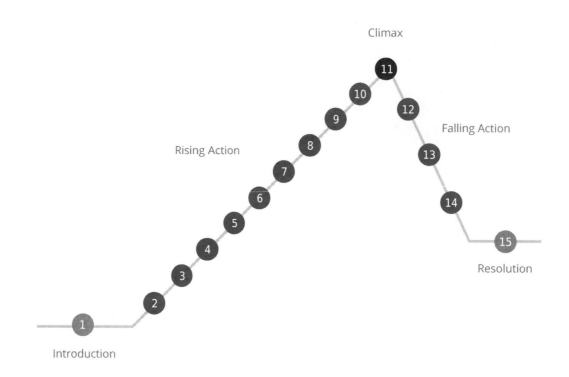

Introduction

1. Mama tells Kambili she is expecting another baby.

Rising Action

2. Papa beats Mama, who miscarries.

3. Kambili and Jaja visit Aunty Ifeoma during Christmas break.

4. Kambili and Jaja are influenced by Ifeoma and her family.

5. Father Amadi and Kambili develop an intense friendship.

6. Papa-Nnukwu comes to Ifeoma's home because he is ill.

7. Papa-Nnukwu dies in Ifeoma's home.

8. Papa burns Kambili for sleeping in a home with Papa-

Nnukwu.

9. Ade Coker is killed by a package bomb.

10. Papa beats Kambili for having a painting of Papa-Nnukwu.

Climax

11. When Jaja refuses Communion, Papa smashes Mama's figurines.

Falling Action

12. Papa dies of rat poison put in his tea by Mama.

13. Confessing to the crime, Jaja is arrested.

 Course Hero

14. Jaja goes to prison, where Mama and Kambili visit him.

Resolution

15. Jaja, after spending three years in prison, will be let out.

Timeline of Events

Friday

Mama reveals she is pregnant and will give birth in October.

The next day

A coup occurs, and the Nigerian government gets a new head of state.

End of the school term

Kambili finishes second in her class on exams, greatly displeasing her father.

Sunday, weeks later

After Papa beats her, Mama miscarries the baby.

Christmas vacation

Kambili and her family spend Christmas in Abba, where she meets her aunt and cousins.

Before Christmas day

Kambili and Jaja go with Aunty Ifeoma to see the mmuo procession, where Igbo men portray spirits.

Day after Christmas

Papa beats Kambili, Jaja, and Mama because Kambili eats before Mass.

Epiphany

Kambili confesses to Father Benedict that she enjoyed looking at the mmuo.

The next day

Kambili and Jaja go to stay with Aunty Ifeoma for a visit.

A day or so later

Papa-Nnukwu goes to stay at Aunty Ifeoma's because he is seriously ill.

The next day

After a pleasant evening, Papa-Nnukwu is found dead in the morning.

Later that day

Papa pours boiling water on Kambili's feet for being in a house with a heathen.

Days later

Ade Coker is killed when a package bomb is delivered to his home and explodes.

Some time later

Papa beats Kambili, almost to the point of death, for having a painting of Papa-Nnukwu.

A few weeks later

Released from the hospital after the beating, Kambili goes to stay with Aunty Ifeoma.

Soon after

Kambili and Father Amadi begin to develop a serious friendship, as he shows affection to her.

Palm Sunday

When Jaja refuses Communion, Papa rages and breaks Mama's figurines.

Good Friday

Kambili learns Aunty Ifeoma is moving to America and Father Amadi is leaving for Germany.

Days later

After confessing to poisoning his father, though Mama is guilty, Jaja is sent to prison.

Three years later

As a result of bribery, Jaja is close to being released from prison.

⌕ Chapter Summaries

Purple Hibiscus has four named parts. This guide further divides each part into sections based on breaks in the narrative, for the purpose of summary and analysis.

Part 1, Section 1

Summary

Kambili, the first-person narrator of the novel, begins by relating what happens on Palm Sunday after her brother Jaja refuses to take Communion at church—after which "things started to fall apart at home." Her father, an extremely devout Catholic, participates intensely during Mass. He is often held up by Father Benedict, the British priest, as an example of devotion and righteousness. Papa is well known in the community for his financial generosity and good works. He has won awards and been featured in magazines for his philanthropy.

Despite his good reputation—or perhaps because of it—Papa is enraged when his son does not go up for Communion. When the family gets home, Papa bangs his missal (the book containing the texts used in the Mass) on the table and confronts his son. Jaja's responses are defiant, and Papa becomes even more enraged, grabbing the missal and hurling it at Jaja. The book misses Jaja but crashes into a group of Mama's small ceramic figurines of ballet dancers. After changing out of her Sunday clothes, Mama comes in and sees the shattered figurines. She begins to pick up the pieces, acting as though nothing important has happened.

Papa pours himself tea, and Kambili waits for him to offer her and Jaja a "love sip," which is his custom. But he does not make his usual offer. He sips his tea. Kambili can't understand why Jaja and Mama are acting as though nothing out of the ordinary is happening. Kambili goes to change her clothes. While upstairs she sits at her bedroom window and looks out at the cashew tree, the hibiscus bushes with their purple and red blossoms, and the walls of the compound. She hears Papa go into his room for a nap. She remembers that government agents once came to visit Papa and had picked blossoms from the hibiscus bushes as they left.

Mama comes in to tell Kambili it is time for lunch. Kambili tells her, "I'm sorry your figurines broke." Kambili knows Mama polishes the figurines each time Papa beats her. At lunch, Papa says a very long prayer of blessing, and then Sisi, the domestic servant, serves lunch. Papa has Sisi bring in a few bottles of cashew juice that were produced in the factory he owns. The family members taste the juice; Mama and Kambili compliment it. Jaja refuses to do what his mother and sister have done and excuses himself from the table. Papa, angered, begins to follow him, but Kambili takes a large drink of cashew juice and begins to cough. Papa and Mama make sure she is well, and the moment of crisis passes.

That evening Kambili develops a fever and stays in bed instead of going down to dinner. When Papa comes up to check on her, she notices his breathing seems labored, and a rash is spreading across his face. Mama brings her some broth, which she vomits. When she asks Mama if she will replace the figurines, Mama says no. Kambili wonders whether this answer is because Mama already knew that when Papa broke the figurines, "it was not just the figurines that came tumbling down, it was everything." Kambili then remembers visiting Aunty Ifeoma in Nsukka and seeing her Aunt's experimental purple hibiscus. In Nsukka, Kambili notes, was when "it all" started. But Kambili can remember further back than that, when the only hibiscus bushes in their front yard were red.

Analysis

The opening section presents most of the main characters, themes, symbols, and important relationships that will populate the story. It also brings a sense of suspense that propels the reader into the past and then back to the present of the story.

Indeed, the first line of the novel is a clue to many issues that will be raised as events unfold. "Things started to fall apart at home when my brother, Jaja, did not go to communion," the narrator tells the reader. This sentence explains what the narrator, Kambili, sees as a turning point both in her life and in the life of her family. Furthermore, it is an important moment because it marks the first overt act of rebellion by Jaja against his father and shows Papa's tendency to react to rebellion with violence. The words "Things started to fall apart" is a reference to the 1958 novel *Things Fall Apart* by Chinua Achebe, another postcolonial Nigerian author who wrote about cultural and religious change, especially the various ways people deal with the intersection of cultures and religions that results from colonialism. Some characters in *Things Fall Apart* resist change, sticking to traditional ways; some embrace the colonial culture and religion; and some blend and adapt Christian and Igbo ways. This dynamic appears as well in *Purple Hibiscus*. Alluding to *Things Fall Apart* also foreshadows the violence with which Papa treats his family, since the main character of Achebe's novel, Okonkwo, is also violent toward his wives and son.

The focus stays on Papa for much of the section. Papa's public and private selves seem to be in conflict, but for Papa they stem from his religious views, which are greatly influenced by Father Benedict and the colonial attitudes of his interpretation of Church teaching. As Aunty Ifeoma says, Papa is "a colonial product." He thinks being civilized means speaking English and shunning his Igbo roots.

The symbols of the figurines, the "love sips," and the purple hibiscus are introduced in the section, though they will come to have more significance as the story progresses. Papa's breaking of the figurines marks a symbolic moment in the life of the family, from which there is no turning back. However, as Kambili realizes at the end of the section, the breaking of the figurines isn't actually the beginning of things falling apart—that started before, at Nsukka. The breaking of the figurines is simply the point at which the change is acknowledged and after which there is no way to pretend the change never happened. The purple hibiscus, already blooming in the garden, is a symbol of this rooted and growing change. Though the nature of the change isn't clear yet, like the purple hibiscus, it originated in Nsukka at Aunty Ifeoma's.

The silence and passivity that are the norm of Kambili's existence are depicted in the family's communication. Interactions are highly ritualized, almost like the Catholic liturgy, or methods of public worship; little room for communication exists outside of those rituals. Papa's love sips are symbolic of his relationship with his family, but they are eerily similar to drinking Communion wine from a common chalice. Prayers are said before and after the meal, and there is the ritual of tasting and complimenting Papa's new product, the cashew juice. Yet, when communication occurs outside of the rituals, it is not straightforward. Most thoughts and feelings go unsaid. Kambili struggles to comfort her mother after the figurines break, but instead of saying, "I am sorry Papa broke your figurines," she says, "I'm sorry your figurines broke." She avoids mentioning the perpetrator to avoid assigning blame.

Hints of the change already happening under the surface appear as well in other section details. For example, the rashes on Papa's face hint that even at this point he is being poisoned and is very unwell. Kambili acknowledges this fact, without revealing the secret: "Maybe Mama had realized that she would not need the figurines anymore."

The last few paragraphs lead the reader into the rest of the novel: Nsukka started it all, and what it started was to begin to "lift the silence" and bring about a kind of freedom. To learn about how the silence was lifted and freedom begun, however, in the next section Kambili must take readers back to a time before Nsukka.

Part 2, Section 2

Summary

Kambili is sitting at her desk, studying, when Mama brings in freshly washed school uniforms. Mama informs her that she is pregnant. Mama is glad she is having another child, because she has miscarried a few times and Papa has been encouraged, by others in the family, to find another wife—one who will bear him more sons. "God works in mysterious ways," Mama says.

Later that evening, the members of Our Lady of the Miraculous Medal prayer group, which Mama hosts, arrive. For half an hour, the house is filled with Igbo songs and hand clapping, followed by a "little something"—an elaborate meal prepared by Mama and Sisi. As the prayer group meets, Jaja comes into Kambili's room and asks what she had for lunch, even though he already knows. Kambili observes they often ask each other questions to which they already know the answer, to avoid asking "the other questions, the ones whose answers we did not want to know." Then Kambili tells Jaja that Mama is pregnant. "We will protect him," he says, and though he doesn't specify from whom, Kambili knows he means to protect the new baby from Papa.

Kambili glances at the detailed schedules Papa has stuck to the wall—one for her and one for Jaja. During the scheduled "family time" the next day, a coup occurs, and a general comes on the radio to announce that a new government has taken over. Papa excuses himself to call Ade Coker, editor of the *Standard*, the newspaper Papa owns. When Papa returns, he speaks about the coup with sadness, noting how coups lead to more coups and result in a vicious cycle of violence and civil war. Papa says what Nigeria needs is a "renewed democracy."

The next day, the family reads about the coup in the newspapers, including Papa's, which is the only paper critical of the new military government. "God will deliver us," Kambili says, wanting to please Papa. Papa agrees and reaches out to hold her hand.

Analysis

As more details of the family's daily life are revealed, so is Papa's tyranny over the minutiae of their routines. Papa's schedules, which allow a specific amount of time for every activity in the day, must be precisely followed. Papa will not tolerate disorder. Even "family time" is on the schedule. According to Papa, the response to any good thing happening is, "Thanks be to God." There are hints, though, that when Papa is not home, Mama, Jaja, and Kambili do relax the rules, just a little. For example, when Mama tells Kambili about her pregnancy, she talks a little more than usual. And when Jaja gets home, he comes into Kambili's room first, because Papa isn't there yet.

But regardless of Papa's presence, silence and avoidance are the characteristics of all communication in Kambili's home. Because speaking what is really in their minds or hearts is not encouraged and the risk of offending Papa comes with consequences, Jaja and Kambili have developed nonverbal ways of communicating. Jaja uses his eyes to say, "I wish we still had lunch together," for example. In addition, expression is limited because the family members don't want to acknowledge Papa's violence, even to themselves. They ask each other questions to which they already know the answers, as a substitute for asking the "other questions," which might be critical of Papa. The vow to protect the new baby, understood as to protect it from Papa, is not said aloud. Kambili makes it clear both she and Jaja are proud of Papa's standing in the community and crave his praise. For her part, Mama is thankful Papa hasn't left her, when other men would have, for failing to have more children. Mama, Jaja, and Kambili are stuck between feelings of pride and gratitude toward Papa and the fear and suffering he causes them.

In the midst of this description of Papa's tyrannical behavior and lack of free expression within his household, the coup

occurs. Papa wants a "renewed democracy" for Nigeria rather than the military rule brought about by the coup. He does not see what is all too apparent to the reader—he rails against the exact sort of rule he maintains in his home. He is prodemocracy, but not with his family. Against the backdrop of this dramatic irony in which the reader knows more than the characters, the coup foreshadows Jaja's rebellion, which is still in the future at this point in the story.

Part 2, Section 3

Summary

Over the next few weeks, the tone of the newspaper coverage changes. Most newspapers become more subdued, but the *Standard* becomes more critical. Soldiers patrol and often stop and search cars. At home Kambili and Jaja continue to follow Papa's schedules, and Mama becomes visibly pregnant.

A visiting priest comes to St. Agnes's to say Mass. He sings an Igbo song during his sermon, and Papa disapproves. After church they go to visit Father Benedict, as is their custom, but when they arrive at Father Benedict's home, Mama says she feels sick and wants to stay in the car. This decision is unacceptable to Papa. He asks her twice "Are you sure you wanted to stay in the car?" She looks at him and changes her mind. After a polite visit with Father Benedict, they return home. Mama is sick. At lunch Papa prays for forgiveness for "those … who had put selfish desires first and had not wanted to visit [God's] servant after Mass." After lunch Kambili hears the sound of Papa beating Mama coming from their room. After the sounds stop, Papa appears, carrying Mama, who is bleeding profusely, over his shoulder. Jaja and Kambili clean up the trail of blood left on the floor. Mama comes home the next day, but she has lost the baby, and her eyes have a vacant look. She polishes the figurines. At dinner Papa announces that the family will recite 16 prayers for forgiveness for Mama. On Sunday they stay after Mass and say the prayers.

Analysis

The coup has changed things outside Kambili's home. However, Papa keeps a tight rein on what happens inside, so the coup hasn't yet affected the everyday lives of Jaja and

Kambili. Papa's will remains law, and even questioning that law is forbidden. After all, Mama gives in and goes into Father Benedict's home for the visit, showing she is obedient. Yet, Papa still beats her and prays that God will forgive her for her sin. It is not enough to do what Papa says. Family members must do what he wants before he says it, because he has equated what he thinks is right with what God thinks is right. If Papa corrects someone, it is already too late—the individual has revealed ignorance of what is right and thus shows a moral failing.

The tense atmosphere in the home caused by Papa's expectations leads Kambili to try constantly to anticipate what Papa will want or like and what will anger him. This guessing game takes up quite a bit of mental space. The dynamic is demonstrated when the young priest begins to sing an Igbo song as part of his sermon. Papa doesn't tell them not to sing, but Jaja and Kambili know Papa's likes and dislikes well, and they are monitoring his reaction to see what theirs should be. Papa purses his lips. They seal their lips as well.

Disdain for the young priest is an important part of Papa's religious orientation. He does not believe the blending of Igbo traditions and culture into Catholic ritual is acceptable. Indeed, he believes bringing in Igbo language and songs is harmful to the Church, even if the songs and language express a Christian message. The young priest gives the first glimpse into another way of being Catholic, and though Papa doesn't appreciate it, Kambili will later in the novel.

Part 2, Section 4

Summary

In the weeks after her mother loses the baby, Kambili finds it difficult to study even though the important first-term exams are approaching. When she looks at her textbooks, all she sees is blood. One night as she is fruitlessly studying, Yewande Coker comes to the house, crying loudly. Ade, her husband, wrote an article implicating the new head of state in drug trafficking and murder and was arrested by soldiers as he was leaving the editorial offices of the *Standard*.

Kambili takes her exams and finishes second in her class. Second is not good enough for Papa, and Kambili knows he will be disappointed. Papa always complained that his "Godless"

father Papa-Nnukwu never spent money on his education, so he sends his children to good schools and expects them to be first in their class. As expected, Papa is not pleased when she informs him that evening of her rank. Dinner is tense, and Kambili has trouble eating. After dinner Papa speaks privately with Kambili and begins to scold her, but he is interrupted by a phone call. He waves at her to leave the room. Kambili expects him to summon her back in, but he never does. Later, Kambili learns that Papa got Ade out of jail, where he had been tortured. Papa decides to take his newspaper underground.

On the Saturday before the beginning of the next term, Mama, Jaja, and Kambili visit the market to buy new sandals, a ritual the three enjoy before the start of every term—even though they don't need new sandals. They see women being beaten by soldiers, who are also destroying the market stands. Kevin, their driver, tells them the soldiers were ordered to destroy the market stalls because they are considered illegal. That Monday Papa drives Kambili to school. Along the way, he throws some money at a beggar, who joyfully receives the cash. The beggar reminds her of one of the women at the market, who cried on the ground in despair.

At school, Sister Margaret, a teacher at Kambili's school, greets them. Papa speaks to her in an English accent, just as he does with Father Benedict. Kambili notes that Papa often uses an English accent when he is talking to white religious people. Papa asks Kambili which of the girls is Chinwe Jideze, who placed first on the exams. He points out that both Chinwe and Kambili have only one head, so there's no reason Kambili should not come in first. She promises him she will not let it happen again.

Another girl, Ezinne, strikes up a conversation with Kambili. As the two discuss their vacations and school, Chinwe comes up to them and asks Ezinne to vote for her for class prefect. Ezinne agrees. Kambili observes Chinwe ask most of the other girls the same thing but skips Kambili. Ezinne says Chinwe is waiting for Kambili to speak to her first, because she thinks Kambili is a snob. In reality, Kambili's hesitance to speak up and her introverted ways are not evidence of arrogance. Ezinne tells her not to run off so quickly after school but to stay and talk with the other girls. Kambili, thinking about the punishment she will receive if she is even a few minutes late, tells Ezinne she simply "likes running."

Analysis

This section again juxtaposes Papa's public persona with his private one. He is quick to respond to the suffering of Ade Coker and his wife, gives money to the poor, and defies the new head of state through his newspaper. Yet, he has caused his own wife to miscarry their child, and the trauma of that event is causing Kambili to hallucinate blood images whenever she looks at her textbooks. Then Papa is disappointed that Kambili did not place first on her exams, even though his own actions caused her failure to achieve top ranking. There's a hint here of a pattern that becomes more evident later in the novel: Papa is the cause of many things that result in his own harm or disappointment. At Kambili's school, Papa shows his public side, as he chats with the staff and speaks graciously, in a British accent, before berating Kambili privately in Igbo about second place.

The incident at the market, when Kambili sees the soldiers ruining the stalls of the poorer women, and the way Papa throws cash at a beggar become linked in Kambili's mind. She sees both the despair of the woman wailing on the ground and the joy of the beggar as the same helplessness. Her awareness of their suffering shows a growing awareness of class and her own privilege. But her thoughts also reveal she understands that both joy and despair can have the same root: helplessness. This duality is one way of understanding Kambili's own ability to feel both pride and fear about Papa, which centers on his role as the authority in her life and on her relative helplessness.

Kambili's situation at school reveals another instance of the theme of public versus private. Her silence and lack of engagement with the other girls are a result of her fear of Papa. She is consumed with doing well on the tests and not being late. But her actions are interpreted in a way that creates a public persona at odds with her real, private self. The other students think she is stuck up because she doesn't talk to them or stay after school to hang out. Of course, Kambili's inability to speak of her fear of Papa, or even admit it, gets in the way of resolving the problem. She can't tell Ezinne why she really needs to run away after school. Papa's tyranny creates a barrier between Kambili and the girls who might have been her friends and confidants, trapping Kambili inside her own silence.

Part 2, Section 5

Summary

Kambili isn't concerned about being seen as a "backyard snob" at school because she is consumed by worry over coming in first on the exams. Still seeing visions of blood every time she looks at her textbooks, she is unable to read. Despite this problem, she does well, and at Christmas break, she comes home with a report card showing her top ranking. Relieved and proud, she basks in her father's praise.

Kambili's family goes to their hometown, Abba, for Christmas. They pray the rosary on the way and are greeted enthusiastically as they drive their expensive cars (the family in one, the servants in the other) through the streets of the town to the tall black gates of their "country home." Throughout the drive and at their arrival, Papa is generous with money—giving money to the children who chase after their car and to the people who sell food along the streets. Such generosity is expected of wealthy families, especially at Christmas. Visitors to the house during the holiday will eat and drink to satisfaction and even take leftovers home.

Ade Coker and his family stop by to wish them a merry Christmas. Ade teases Jaja and Kambili about being bored in the small village, far from friends. Kambili and Jaja just smile, prompting Coker to remark on how quiet they are. "Imagine what the *Standard* would be if we were all quiet," he jokes. Papa doesn't laugh.

The next day Jaja and Kambili wake up and go downstairs for morning prayers. Papa prays especially for the conversion of his own father, Papa-Nnukwu, so that Papa-Nnukwu will not go to hell. After the prayers, Papa tells the children they may visit Papa-Nnukwu for 15 minutes, as long as they do not touch or eat anything while in his home. This visit is a concession to pressure from the extended family to allow Papa-Nnukwu to know his grandchildren, even if he still practices his traditional religion and refuses to become Catholic.

Kevin drives the children to Papa-Nnukwu's home, where the elderly man greets them and offers them food. They, of course, refuse. He also tells them Aunty Ifeoma and her children are coming to visit, arriving tomorrow. He says it is a shame they do not know their cousins. Kambili knows this tension in the family is over Papa's refusal to allow his father into his home unless he converts to Catholicism. Kambili reflects on the difference between how Papa treats Papa-Nnukwu and how he treated his Catholic and westernized father-in-law, known to Kambili as Grandfather, before his death. Papa would praise Grandfather, saying, "He did things the right way, the way the white people did, not what our people do now!"

Later that afternoon, Kambili watches as her father angrily shouts at an old man named Anikwenwa, whom he calls "a worshipper of idols," and has him escorted out of the compound.

Analysis

The section begins with a reminder of Kambili's fragile emotional state. She is still traumatized by her mother's beating and miscarriage, yet despite Papa's terrible violence she still feels validation when he praises her for doing well in school.

Then the setting changes to the village of Abba—the hometown of Papa's extended family, or *umunna*. The wealth of Kambili's family is even more apparent in the small village of Abba than in the larger city of Enugu. Thus, Papa's generosity toward those less fortunate is also more apparent. They arrive in Abba with two expensive cars packed to the brim with food to make a Christmas feast. Papa—who holds the traditional title *omelora*, meaning "one who does for the community"—throws cash at the poor children, telling them to tell their parents where it came from. Not content merely to do good works, Papa wants to be seen doing good works. This desire for attention suggests his motive for being philanthropic is more about appearances than generosity.

In this section it becomes more evident that Papa's embrace of a strict version of Catholicism is in large part a result of his belief that white people are more civilized than his own Igbo people—they "do things the right way." Papa rejects not only Igbo traditional religion but also Igbo influence on the Catholic religion, even though many Igbo people have become Catholic. Papa's unyielding belief in white supremacy has led to the severing of family ties and a rejection of any part of his father's religion. The novel definitely presents Papa's dogmatic and inflexible religion in a negative light, though it does not treat all of Catholicism negatively. Papa has allowed his religious belief to erode family relationships that are important to traditional

Igbo life. He is overly concerned about avoiding hell, suggesting his own religious education focused more on sin and hell than on love and joy.

Ade Coker's visit includes an awkward moment when Ade notices Jaja and Kambili are unusually quiet. He unwittingly puts his finger on the contradiction between Papa's public behavior and his private life as he notes the *Standard* depends on not being quiet. While Papa is not amused, the reader can't help but wish, for Kambili's sake, that Papa would apply his feelings about freedom and democracy to his own life.

Part 2, Section 6

Summary

When Aunty Ifeoma arrives the next day, she greets Kambili with a big hug and playful teasing. Uncomfortable with Aunty Ifeoma's exuberance, Kambili is polite. When Mama comes in, she and Ifeoma make conversation. One bit of conversation is Ifeoma's revelation that her late husband's family believe she killed him and is hiding the money he left, which is a ridiculous idea. Mama says that sometimes *umunna*, or extended family on the male line, say hurtful things, such as encouraging Papa to find a new wife to bear him more children. Ifeoma tells her being left wouldn't have been so bad, because "sometimes life begins when marriage ends." Mama scoffs at this "university talk."

Aunty Ifeoma also shares the news that times are tough in Nsukka because of the military government and fuel shortage. The university at which Ifeoma teaches is unable to pay its lecturers, who are beginning to leave and go to America to find jobs as adjunct professors.

When Papa arrives, Aunty Ifeoma suggests that Kambili and Jaja spend some time with her and her children. When Papa seems reluctant, Aunty Ifeoma becomes insistent, and Kambili is surprised to hear anyone talking to Papa in that way. But he gives in, cautioning Ifeoma to keep his children away from anything ungodly. Then Papa invites them to have lunch together on Christmas Day.

Soon after Papa leaves, Ifeoma's children arrive: Amaka—Ifeoma's daughter—and Obiora and Chima, Ifeoma's sons. They are far more outgoing than Kambili, laughing easily and loudly. When Amaka asks if they can watch television, Kambili says they don't watch a lot of television. Amaka thinks Kambili is replying in a stuck-up way, as if Kambili were so bored with satellite television she doesn't find it interesting anymore. However, Kambili knows they don't watch television because Papa doesn't put it into their schedules.

Aunty Ifeoma arrives at the house as they are finishing breakfast the next day. Papa has consented to let the children spend the day with their aunt and cousins. Aunty Ifeoma invites Mama to come along, but Mama says Papa likes her to stay around the home. Ifeoma also suggests that Kambili wear trousers, but Kambili says she's fine—inwardly wondering why she doesn't just tell her aunt she owns no trousers because it is sinful for a woman to wear them.

Once Kambili and Jaja drive off with Ifeoma and her children, Ifeoma says they are going to stop and pick up Papa-Nnukwu. Jaja and Kambili glance at each other, knowing their grandfather's presence would not be fine with Papa and fearful of how he would react. At Papa-Nnukwu's, they refuse to go in to greet him, saying they are not allowed to because Papa-Nnukwu is a pagan. Ifeoma scoffs at this remark, saying he is a traditionalist, not a pagan. Aunty Ifeoma and her children laugh and joke with Papa-Nnukwu after he gets in the car, but Kambili and Jaja remain mostly silent.

Aunty Ifeoma takes them to the festival at Ezi Icheke, where they watch a procession of *mmuo*—men in masks that represent Igbo spirits. Afterward, Ifeoma takes them back home. That night Kambili dreams she is laughing, and even though she doesn't know what her laughter sounds like, in the dream it sounds like Aunty Ifeoma's.

Analysis

Aunty Ifeoma emerges in this section as a larger-than-life figure. She walks fast, talks fast, and laughs loudly. She shocks Kambili by arguing with Papa. She also fascinates Kambili, who is captivated by "the fearlessness about her, about the way she gestured as she spoke, the way she smiled." As the section progresses, Aunty Ifeoma's fearlessness is demonstrated in a number of ways, but there is one way Kambili finds most intriguing: she is not afraid of Papa.

Aunty Ifeoma is a foil for Papa—she's as tall and confident as he is but her outlook on religion and gender roles contrast

Papa's. She is also a foil for Mama, telling Mama that life can begin when marriage ends and inviting Mama to ride along in the car. Mama brushes away both suggestions. For Kambili, being around Aunty Ifeoma challenges her concept of religion, her view of her father, and her ideas about womanly behavior. These challenges are hard for Kambili to confront because they make her uncomfortable and cause her to act overly politely. But they do seem to have a lasting impact on Kambili's consciousness; in her dream her laughter sounds like her aunt's. Simply being around Aunty Ifeoma for a short time has planted the seeds of future freedom, to smile and laugh, in Kambili. The dream also underscores Kambili's lack of laughter, because she doesn't know what her own laugh sounds like.

This section also explores the harm Papa's attitude toward Papa-Nnukwu has had on his children. As Jaja and Kambili accompany Aunty Ifeoma, their cousins, and Papa-Nnukwu to see the *mmuo*, they keenly feel their separation from the rest of their family. Kambili doesn't know how Papa-Nnukwu's stories "go on and on," and because Jaja has not done the *ima mmuo*, or initiation into the spirit world, he makes a mistake in etiquette at the procession of the *mmuo*. Papa has raised his children completely apart from the traditional religion, and while he thinks he is saving them from sin, he has actually stolen something precious from them—a sense of connection to the past through family and tradition. Aunty Ifeoma seems to honor and humor the traditional beliefs, even though she too is a Catholic. But she allows her children to stay in touch with their culture and traditions.

The silence that dominates Jaja and Kambili's lives at home makes it even harder for them to connect with their extended family. They communicate their discomfort by exchanging glances, not by speaking up. They mumble and stumble when they are asked questions about their lives. This behavior leads Amaka, like the girls at Kambili's school, to think that Jaja and Kambili are snobbish. Kambili doesn't know how to explain that she doesn't own trousers and isn't allowed to watch satellite television. Amaka fills the silence with her own assumptions, based on the knowledge that Kambili's family is wealthier than hers. This misunderstanding serves to exacerbate the isolation Kambili feels.

Part 2, Section 7

Summary

Kambili's family attends Christmas Mass, but Papa is disappointed in the priest. After Mass, they go to a fundraiser for the priest's new house, and Papa makes a generous donation. Later, with the house full of Christmas visitors, Papa shakes hands and chats while Jaja and Kambili go with Mama to welcome the wives of the *umunna*. The women fuss over the children briefly, and then Mama tells Jaja and Kambili to go upstairs and change clothes.

Hearing her cousins and aunt laughing, Kambili goes into the living room, breathing steadily to avoid stuttering with nervousness. Obiora and Amaka put on some music and wonder at the stereo, and Chima marvels at the amenities in the bathroom. Then the Igwe, the traditional ruler of Abba, arrives. While Papa visits with the Igwe, Mama and Aunty Ifeoma talk privately, though Kambili overhears. Mama tells Aunty Ifeoma that there are cylinders of gas at one of Papa's factories and that she should ask Papa for some gas. Aunty Ifeoma tells her she knows there would be strings attached to such a gift. Then she tells Mama that Papa never liked her husband Ifediora because Ifediora told him truths he did not want to hear. She thinks Papa is cruel not to let his own father, who is old and sick, into his house. She says that Papa should stop trying to do God's job. "God is big enough to do his own job ... let God do the judging."

At lunch Aunty Ifeoma suggests Papa should let Kambili and Jaja visit with her and their cousins in Nsukka. The two argue about it for a while, and the topic is tabled. Amaka mentions that a small village in Benue is experiencing apparitions, or sightings, of the Virgin Mary. Ifeoma chimes in that she could take all of the cousins on a pilgrimage there, if Papa will let Kambili and Jaja visit her for a week during their vacation. This idea wins him over, and he agrees to the visit.

The next morning, a Sunday, Kambili gets her period. With it come severe cramps. Mama tells her to quickly eat a few cornflakes so she can take medicine for the cramps, even though eating the cereal breaks the fast they must keep for an hour before taking Communion. Jaja pours the cereal for her. Unfortunately, Papa catches them. Mama tries to explain, and Jaja claims he, not Mama, told Kambili to eat the cornflakes. Papa takes off his belt and whips all three of them with it. Afterward, he asks them, "Why do you like to sin?" They change their clothes, wash their faces, and go to Mass.

After New Year's Day, Kambili's family leaves Abba. Two days later, on Epiphany, "a holy day of obligation," the family goes to see Father Benedict for confession, or Reconciliation. Kambili goes last and tells Father Benedict about looking at the *mmuo*. He asks whether she enjoyed it, and she says yes. He then assigns her penance for her sin. On the ride home Papa is bright eyed and smiling as he says, "I am spotless now, we are all spotless." He tells Jaja and Kambili to pack their things for five days with Aunty Ifeoma. Mama notes they should not go empty-handed and casually suggests they send some cylinders of gas.

The next morning they set off, driven by Kevin, with two gas cylinders and Papa's schedules made specially for the week. Before they leave, Papa hugs them and says, "I have never been without you two for more than a day." They see Papa waving and crying as they drive away.

Analysis

This section provides deeper insight into Papa, making him if not sympathetic, at least more human. A great deal of Papa's behavior is familiar by this time, such as giving money to charity in public ways while privately abusing and terrorizing his wife and children. The earnest joy Papa feels after confession, when he feels free of sin, gives insight into the deep sense of guilt and unworthiness that must drive his behavior. In the same way, Papa's emotional goodbye as Jaja and Kambili leave for Nsukka shows he doesn't know how to be away from them. It may be difficult for readers not to feel bad for Papa as he cries and waves at his children. Yet Papa, only the day before, brutally beat his whole family because Kambili ate a few cornflakes to take medicine before Mass. He has made them schedules for the week because he can't give up his sense of control over them. He is a hurt and broken person, as many abusers are.

Yet, the section also shows how Papa's tyranny fosters conspiracy and plotting against him. Like all tyrants, Papa's own heavy-handed enforcement means others conspire to resist his absolute control. Readers may recall that not long ago, Papa decided to take his paper underground. It turns out that an underground of sorts actually exists in Papa's own family. First, Aunty Ifeoma and Mama privately discuss that Papa has several gas cylinders at one of his factories. Ifeoma knows asking outright means strings will be attached. So, Mama formulates a different plan. She appeals to the custom of not arriving at someone's house empty-handed and nonchalantly suggests Ifeoma might really appreciate fuel, which is in short supply in Nsukka. Papa then sends the gas cylinders to his sister. As another example, Aunty Ifeoma and Amaka seem to team up to convince Papa that Kambili and Jaja should visit them, using Papa's religious devotion against him as they argue that they will go to the village in Benue to see the apparitions of the Virgin Mary. Unfortunately, not every conspiracy is successful. Mama, Jaja, and Kambili conspire to make sure Kambili can take her pain medication when she has menstrual cramps, and Papa catches them. Punishment follows.

Worthy of note, too, is the way Jaja tries to take responsibility for Kambili's breaking the fast. Though he did encourage Kambili to eat and take the medicine, both Mama and Kambili were willing participants in the deception. Jaja's version of protecting his loved ones involves martyrdom, in hopes that the punishment will fall on him and not his loved ones. This is an important aspect of his personality.

Part 2, Section 8

Summary

Aunty Ifeoma's apartment is small and shabby, but it has a colorful garden and smells of curry and nutmeg. After Kevin leaves to go back to Enugu, Aunty Ifeoma makes Jaja and Kambili welcome as she cooks, talks, and laughs. Shortly after, Amaka, Obiora, and Chima arrive. Kambili goes with Amaka to the room they will share during the visit. Amaka still thinks that Kambili looks down on her because Kambili is wealthy in comparison. After a few awkward questions and Kambili's halting answers, Amaka asks, "Why do you lower your voice? ... You talk in whispers." Kambili doesn't have a good answer. Amaka plays a music cassette and asks Kambili about her taste in music. Kambili doesn't know how to tell her she doesn't own a cassette player and doesn't know anything about pop music.

Back in the kitchen, Amaka fries plantains, and the boys come in with soft drinks. Obiora sets the table. After a short prayer, they begin to eat lunch. Ifeoma's family is full of laughter and nonstop conversation, but Kambili struggles to eat and is mostly silent during the meal. After lunch Papa calls. He

reminds Kambili to study and pray every day, and Kambili wonders if he can tell from her voice she said a "too short prayer" before dinner.

Later that evening Aunty Ifeoma tells them her family says the rosary after dinner, but afterward they can watch television as long as they like. Jaja notes that Papa's schedule indicates they have to study in the evenings. Aunty Ifeoma is astounded Papa has sent schedules and demands Jaja and Kambili give them to her. She takes the schedules to her room and tells her guests they will follow her house rules while they are in her house. Even without her schedule, however, Kambili still feels its power over her, and she goes to bed at the time she knows Papa indicated.

The next day Aunty Ifeoma wants to take Kambili and Jaja on a tour of the university. On the way out, Jaja notices purple hibiscus in her garden—not the typical red. When he asks about the color, she tells him her friend Phillipa, a botanist, does experimental work with flowers. She created the purple hibiscus along with several other unusual flowers. Jaja is entranced.

They drive around Nsukka and the university, taking in the buildings and grounds, as Aunty Ifeoma acts as tour guide. They return to Aunty Ifeoma's home to make lunch. Father Amadi, a young priest in town, has been invited to eat with them. When he arrives, Kambili is surprised he is wearing a T-shirt and faded jeans. In the course of the meal's conversation, Kambili realizes he is the young priest who visited St. Agnes and sang in Igbo during his sermon. When Father Amadi realizes Eugene Achike (Papa) is Ifeoma's brother, he notes that the *Standard* is the only paper telling the truth now and that Papa will be getting an award from *Amnesty World*.

After dinner they say their evening prayers and watch television. Father Amadi asks Kambili why she has not smiled or laughed. Ifeoma says Kambili is shy. Kambili abruptly gets up and goes to bed.

Analysis

Contrasts between Kambili's household and Aunty Ifeoma's household make up most of this section. Aunty Ifeoma's family prays at the same times that Papa does, but the prayers are shorter, punctuated by Igbo songs, and include requests for joy and laughter. Aunty Ifeoma allows argument and debate at the dinner table, and the home is always filled with laughter and talk. Kambili is used to tight controls on what can be said and is amazed by the freedom Aunty Ifeoma's family enjoys. Family members say anything they want, listen to music when they want, and watch television as long as they like in the evenings.

There are other, more physical, differences as well. The apartment floors are rough cement, while at home Kambili's floors are smooth marble. The bathroom is smaller and more rustic than at Kambili's home, and water must be fetched each morning for bathing. Dining chairs and plates are mismatched, the food is plain, and the furniture is old. Everyone helps with the cooking and other chores, as there are no household servants to cook and clean.

These differences make Kambili feel out of place to the point at which she feels as though she isn't physically present. Instead, she feels as if she were watching a place where "the air was free for you to breathe as you wished." This feeling is most pronounced when Aunty Ifeoma takes Papa's schedules away. Sitting and watching television with the others, Kambili feels as though it is her shadow visiting Aunty Ifeoma, not her real self. Kambili says her real self is "studying in my room in Enugu, my schedule posted above me."

The more Kambili feels out of place, the quieter she becomes. She struggles to express even the most basic thoughts or ask the most basic questions, such as how to flush the toilet. Jaja is having some of the same issues, and the two use their wordless communication to share their discomfort. When Aunty Ifeoma's family says the rosary, they sing Igbo songs after every section. Jaja clearly wants to join in and communicates this desire with his eyes, "watery, full of suggestions." Kambili tells him *no* with a blink of her eyes, thinking of what Papa would say: "You d[o] not break into song in the middle of the rosary."

The symbolic significance of the purple hibiscus is developed in this section. Ifeoma tells them that it is experimental and unusual but blossoms well. In contrast to the common red hibiscus, the purple is new and different. Because of these qualities, it represents possibility and newness, a way to live vibrantly without following traditional rules. The text links Jaja with the purple hibiscus. He sees it first, just as he is first to begin opening up and talking more freely. He asks about it and then comments on its beauty. Notably, it blooms "close to the barbed wire fencing," foreshadowing an important event in Jaja's character arc. It blossoms and grows freely despite

being behind a barbed wire fence.

Part 2, Section 9

Summary

Kambili still feels out of place at Aunty Ifeoma's, where the laughter, arguing, and singing fill the small space and constantly remind Kambili of the quiet spaciousness of her own home. Some of the tasks Kambili is asked to do, such as washing dishes and peeling yams, she does not do well. Amaka makes fun of her and teases her about her "fancy" schedule. When Amaka's school friends come over, Kambili feels even more out of place. When she is asked about her hair, she coughs, unable to answer that her long, thick hair is all her own.

Kambili's behavior prompts Amaka to ask Ifeoma if Jaja and Kambili are abnormal. But Ifeoma has little patience for this rudeness. In truth, Jaja seems to be acclimating somewhat to Ifeoma's family. He helps tend the garden, talks with Aunty Ifeoma, and even engages in conversation with his cousins. In a conversation about Jaja's name, Ifeoma mentions King Jaja of Opobo, who defied the British. She notes that defiance is not always bad or wrong, seeming to direct this statement at Jaja. Kambili notices that Jaja is taking part more and more in conversations with Ifeoma's family. Chima asks Jaja about his little finger, which is misshapen, and Aunty Ifeoma says it was caused by an accident. Kambili knows the old injury was Papa's punishment for failing to come in first in Holy Communion class. As she glances at Ifeoma, she realizes Ifeoma knows this too. She is shocked that Jaja has revealed this secret.

Mama calls with news: the offices of the *Standard* were ransacked and destroyed by soldiers of the Nigerian head of state, and Ade Coker was arrested. Papa calls later to tell Ifeoma that Kambili and Jaja can stay with her a few more days. The next day Father Amadi visits and offers to bring Jaja, Obiora, and Kambili to play soccer with some of the local boys. Noticing that Ifeoma seems dejected, Father Amadi asks what is wrong. Ifeoma says that Papa-Nnukwu is ill and she doesn't have enough gas in the car to bring him to her home. Father Amadi offers to help get gas. Kambili worries about what will happen if Papa-Nnukwu comes to stay at Ifeoma's house and Papa finds out his children have slept in the same house as a heathen. The next day Ifeoma takes Obiora and goes to get

Papa-Nnukwu.

When Papa-Nnukwu arrives, he greets everyone weakly and goes to take a nap. Later that day, Doctor Nduoma arrives to examine Papa-Nnukwu. Kambili asks Jaja whether Papa will find out Papa-Nnukwu is staying there and whether he told Ifeoma about how his finger became deformed. When he confirms he did, Kambili is taken aback by Jaja's openness and lack of concern about Papa's reactions.

That evening Papa-Nnukwu seems jolly as he eats and takes his medicine. When the electricity unexpectedly goes out, he entertains the family with a traditional Igbo story about how the tortoise cracked its shell, a story whose moral warns against greed and selfishness. Kambili can't see what is wrong about the stories, which seem harmless. But she knows Papa disapproves of them, so she does not laugh along with the others.

Analysis

Kambili and Jaja seem to be growing apart, as Jaja fits in more with Aunty Ifeoma and her family and Kambili remains an outsider. Kambili still lives in constant fear of Papa, while Jaja brushes off her fears and worries. Kambili is so uncomfortable that she can hardly get words out of her mouth, whereas Jaja begins to tell Aunty Ifeoma about himself. A major development is the conversation about Jaja's deformed finger. Kambili is shocked to learn Jaja has told Aunty Ifeoma that Papa is the one who crushed his finger. She is shocked not simply because he told someone but because he spoke about it at all. This was information both Kambili and Jaja knew but would never acknowledge in words, even to each other. So not only has Jaja revealed their secret, he has voiced something never spoken aloud before. "Had Jaja forgotten that we never told, that there was so much that we never told?" she wonders.

Aunty Ifeoma subtly encourages Jaja to resist Papa's abuse and tyranny, reminding him of the "defiant king" Jaja Opobo, who resisted the British takeover of trade. Saying "being defiant can be a good thing," she looks at Jaja and speaks in a noticeably solemn tone. In suggesting Opobo as a role model for Jaja and implying that a little defiance against Papa could be a good thing, Aunty Ifeoma casts Papa in the role of British colonist. This attitude is in keeping with her assessment of Papa as a "colonial product" and her criticism of his controlling ways.

The arrival of Papa-Nnukwu is an unexpected development that increases tension in the story. Readers know Papa eventually will find out he was there, as Kambili fears, and will punish his children violently. Yet, this consequence seems unavoidable, as Papa-Nnukwu is ill and the only right thing for Ifeoma to do is to bring him to her home and care for him. Despite this ominous sense of future trouble, Papa-Nnukwu's presence is a healing one for Jaja. He gets to hear his grandfather's stories and take part in the laughter and fun that, so far in his life, he has not been free to do. However, Kambili does not feel free to join in the chanting with the other family members or speak with her grandfather, which is significant because it shows how Kambili doesn't engage in her own life. She is not living her own experience because she is afraid of the consequences from her father. She has internalized his oppression much in the way Papa has internalized the oppression he experiences from the colonists.

The symbol of the purple hibiscus and its connection to Jaja's emerging sense of freedom is expanded in this section. When Kambili notices Jaja talking more during conversations with Ifeoma and the cousins, she observes the light in his eyes she first noticed when he saw the purple hibiscus. Both Kambili and Jaja recognize that the purple hibiscus represents a new way of being in the world, and even though that way is unfamiliar, it is beautiful. It is the freedom of possibility, a hope for a future.

Part 2, Section 10

Summary

The next day Father Amadi stops by to check on Papa-Nnukwu. Kambili finds her hands shaking and her eyes drawn to Father Amadi's "comfortable gait." Father Amadi invites her and the others to play soccer at the stadium later that day. But when he returns, she pretends to be napping. When she comes out from her nap, Amaka is painting a picture of Papa-Nnukwu, and Ifeoma is preparing food. Ifeoma notes how well Papa-Nnukwu is doing, praising Our Lady for helping to bring him to better health. Kambili asks how Our Lady can help a heathen, and Ifeoma says Papa is a traditionalist, not a heathen. As Ifeoma talks, Kambili hears Amaka and Papa-Nnukwu laughing in the other room.

Aunty Ifeoma wakes Kambili up at dawn the next day and tells her to go watch Papa-Nnukwu on the veranda. Papa-Nnukwu is completing a morning prayer ritual. Kambili notices that he prays for Papa. Later that morning, as Ifeoma gets ready to go to the market, she asks Kambili to prepare the *orah* leaves to make soup. Kambili does not know how, and Amaka criticizes her: "Why? ... Because rich people do not prepare *orah* in their houses?" When Kambili does not respond to this insult, Ifeoma becomes exasperated, saying "Have you no mouth? Talk back to her!" Kambili finally responds, saying she doesn't know how but Amaka can show her. Amaka laughs and says, "So your voice can be this loud, Kambili."

Later that day Kambili agrees to go to the stadium with Father Amadi. She borrows a pair of Amaka's shorts to wear and briefly tries on Amaka's lipstick before wiping it off. At the stadium, Father Amadi and Kambili race, and he tells her she has "good legs for running." He also notes that she never smiles. He notices the wiped-off lipstick on her hand, and his questions about it show that he knows today was the first day she tried to wear lipstick. As she realizes this, Kambili smiles.

Several boys arrive to play soccer with Father Amadi, and Kambili watches them. On the way back to Aunty Ifeoma's home, Kambili asks him why he became a priest. "I had many questions, growing up," he answers. "The priesthood came closest to answering them." Kambili thinks it is a shame that his good looks will not be passed down to any children.

When Kambili returns to Aunty Ifeoma's, she learns Papa has found out that Papa-Nnukwu is staying there and that he is angry. Ifeoma has promised to bring Jaja and Kambili home the day after tomorrow. Kambili goes to bed worrying about what Papa will do.

The next morning Papa-Nnukwu is found dead. Shortly after the body is taken to the morgue, Papa arrives. When he finds out Papa-Nnukwu is dead, he insists that he has a Catholic funeral, a request that puts Aunty Ifeoma in a rage. Refusing to take part in pagan rituals, Papa tells Jaja and Kambili to pack quickly and come with him. As Kambili leaves, Amaka secretly slips her the unfinished painting of Papa-Nnukwu. Kambili hides it in her bag.

When they get home, they see that Mama's face is bruised. They inform her that Papa-Nnukwu is dead, and Papa complains that Ifeoma didn't even call a priest before he died, because he might have converted. When Jaja suggests that he may not have wanted to convert, Papa glowers, and at dinner, when Jaja asks for the key to his room so that he can have

some privacy, Papa accuses him of wanting to masturbate. Kambili wonders why Jaja even asked for the key, when they both know Papa never would allow them to lock their doors.

A little while later Papa calls out for Kambili to get into bathtub. Expecting to be lashed with a stick, Kambili doesn't understand why she should stand in the tub. But she obeys. Papa weeps and says she saw "sin and ... walked right into it." Then he pours boiling water into the tub, saying, "This is what you do ... when you walk into sin. You burn yourself." Kambili screams in pain, and Mama comes in, also weeping. She makes a salt poultice to put on Kambili's feet and gives her pain pills as she tucks her into bed. Kambili touches the hidden painting of Papa-Nnukwu as she lies in bed. After Papa comes in to tell her that what he did was for her own good, she thinks of the painting again.

The next day she reveals the painting to Jaja, and he shows her a bundle of purple hibiscus plants Aunty Ifeoma sent home with them for their own garden. At lunch, Papa tells them he sent Ifeoma the money for Papa-Nnukwu's traditional funeral, even though he disapproves of it. As they are eating, Ade Coker stops by, bringing another man with him, to talk with Papa. Ade tells Papa that the head of state, whom he refers to as Big Oga, will give an interview to the *Standard* in exchange for the newspaper's killing a story about Nwankiti Ogechi, a democratic activist who has disappeared. Ade does not want to comply. Government agents come see Papa that night, attempting to bribe him into compliance.

Kambili sees the next edition of the *Standard*, featuring a cover story about Nwankiti Ogechi, claiming he has been murdered and implicating the government in the murder. Over the next few days, several men belonging to the Democratic Coalition visit Papa, who is now in danger from the government because of the story. Aunty Ifeoma calls to check on Papa, and Jaja speaks with her. In the conversation, he mentions he's planted the purple hibiscus. She notes that Father Amadi often asks about Jaja and Kambili. Amaka and Kambili also talk for a while on the phone. Amaka wants Kambili to come for her confirmation. When Kambili asks what name Amaka will choose for her confirmation, Amaka doesn't answer.

Later, alone in her room, Kambili writes "Father Amadi" all over a piece of paper, and over the next few weeks, she continues to write his name and think about him.

Analysis

There is a lot to unpack in this very long section. Kambili's growing infatuation with Father Amadi weaves in and out of the other plot events. Early in the section her eye is captivated by his "comfortable gait." Later, he holds her hand and appreciates her strong legs. By the end of the section, she is recalling fondly his compliments and girlishly writing his name over and over on a sheet of paper. In many ways these are painfully normal experiences for a 15-year-old young woman to have, even though the object of her affection is a young priest who has taken a vow of celibacy. However, the rest of Kambili's life is not so sweetly mundane. The bruises on Mama's face and the burning of Kambili's feet with boiling water are terrible reminders of the pain that Kambili, Jaja, and Mama are hiding.

The tension between traditional Igbo religion and colonial religion/Catholicism is also developed in this section. In one conversation Papa-Nnukwu asks Father Amadi, who will soon leave to do missionary work elsewhere, not to teach people to "disregard their fathers." Papa-Nnukwu's own experience was that his son (Papa), taught by missionaries, then rejected not only his father's religion but his father personally. This complaint becomes more poignant when Papa refuses at first to have anything to do with giving his father a traditional rather than a Catholic funeral. Shunning Papa-Nnukwu in life is one thing, but shunning him in death seems even crueler. Evidently, this attitude crosses an internal boundary for Papa, who eventually backs down from his stance and decides at least to pay for the funeral.

Papa's disdain for the Igbo religion causes a moral dilemma for Kambili as well. She tells Father Amadi that she is sleeping in the same house with a heathen—her grandfather—believing such proximity to be a sin. When Father Amadi asks her why she thinks it is a sin, she concedes that it is because her father says so. Father Amadi clearly disagrees, and although his opinion doesn't fully resolve Kambili's conflict, it shows her there are ways other than Papa's of practicing Catholicism.

Kambili's understanding of how Igbo traditional religion and Catholicism might live in peace together, as Father Amadi implies, is furthered through Aunty Ifeoma's intervention. Ifeoma prays for the Virgin Mary to help heal Papa-Nnukwu, and Kambili asks how Our Lady can help a heathen. Ifeoma replies that Papa-Nnukwu is a traditionalist, not a heathen. Later, Aunty Ifeoma contrives to allow Kambili to witness Papa-Nnukwu at his morning prayers, likely hoping Kambili will see

his practices are not so different from Catholic practices. Kambili notices he prays for forgiveness and for the health and well-being of his family. Such prayers are not unlike those of Papa, Ifeoma, and other Catholics.

The symbols of the purple hibiscus and the painting of Papa-Nnukwu help tie the section's many threads together. The purple hibiscus is a symbol of freedom and subversion, whereas the painting of Papa-Nnukwu represents the longing Kambili feels for connection with her extended family. Both are items Jaja and Kambili bring home from Aunty Ifeoma's, and each represents something of which Papa will disapprove. As such, they take on additional meaning as symbols of resistance.

Part 2, Section 11

Summary

Ade Coker is killed when a package bomb is delivered to him at home and explodes as he opens it. When Jaja and Kambili get home from school, they find Papa sobbing and Mama comforting him. Papa organizes Ade's funeral, buys Ade's wife and children a new home, and gives time off and bonuses to the *Standard* staff. Dark circles appear under his eyes. Fearing for Papa's safety, Kambili begins having nightmares. Although no direct attempts on Papa's life occur, the government makes subtler attacks. Soldiers bring dead rats to one of Papa's factories, claim they found them there, and close it down for health code violations.

One day Jaja comes to Kambili's room and asks to see the painting of Papa-Nnukwu. He assures Kambili that Papa is with Father Benedict and will not catch them. Kambili takes the painting from the bag in which she keeps it, and Jaja admires it. They look at the painting for a long time. Kambili imagines Papa coming in and finding them looking at the painting, yet they continue to look at it. And then Papa does come in and discovers what they were doing. Both Jaja and Kambili claim responsibility. Snatching the painting, Papa shreds it, throwing the pieces on the floor. Kambili falls to the floor on top of the pieces and lies there. When Papa tells her to get up, she does not obey. He begins to kick her and doesn't stop beating her until she falls unconscious.

She wakes up, in terrible pain, in the hospital. Father Benedict comes to give her extreme unction (anointing of the sick). Papa and Mama are both there. Father Amadi comes to visit, as do Kambili's classmates and Aunty Ifeoma. Through the pain and medication, Kambili hears her aunt say, "When a house is on fire, you run out before the roof collapses on your head." Ifeoma insists that Kambili and Jaja come to stay with her in Nsukka. After a time, Kambili is discharged from the hospital and learns Aunty Ifeoma has convinced Papa to let her go to Nsukka—agreeing with her that "Nsukka air would be good for ... recuperation."

Analysis

The weather at the beginning of this section is described as "a strange, furious rain." In keeping with this angry and violent setting, the section begins with one of the most violent actions yet in the novel. Ade Coker is killed by a package bomb while sitting at the breakfast table with his wife and children. The peaceful domestic scene that is interrupted by the bomb's explosion is described in great detail. Ade's older daughter is sitting across the table in her school uniform, and his wife is feeding the baby in a high chair. The sweetness of the moment just before his death adds to the emotional impact of this event.

The bad weather continues as this scene transitions to the next, in which Jaja and Kambili arrive home from school. They are "almost drenched" as they go from the car to the front door, and when they arrive home Papa is weeping—drenching himself in his own tears. The intensity of the weather reflects Papa's emotions.

In Kambili's nightmares she sees Ade Coker's daughter and his charred remains. Sometimes she becomes his daughter and the charred remains are Papa's. Although these nightmares are sparked by Kambili's fear that her father will also be murdered, her dreams also foreshadow Papa's fate.

The most significant event in this section, however, is Kambili and Jaja's act of defiance in looking at, and lingering over, the painting of Papa-Nnukwu. They both know that if Papa catches them, the consequences will be serious. They know this, and nevertheless they still look at the painting. Jaja examines it closely, touching it lovingly with his deformed finger. As time passes, Papa's catching them becomes inevitable. Kambili explains that maybe she and Jaja wanted to be caught. She thinks the changes made in all of them at Nsukka were already

set, so things "were destined to not be the same, to not be in their original order." Sensing this transition on some level, they look at the painting too long so that the deep changes might be brought into the open and inevitable conflict precipitated. This idea is an echo of Kambili's statement in the novel's opening section that the changes symbolized by the breaking of the figurines began long before, at Nsukka. This scene, then, confirms that the taste of freedom they enjoyed at Aunty Ifeoma's has made it impossible for them to go all the way back to the subjugation of Papa's control. Thus, Jaja's defiance of Papa on Palm Sunday is not his first act of defiance.

The pattern of Jaja's self-sacrifice continues when Papa finds them with the painting, as Jaja immediately claims the painting is his. However, Kambili beats him at his own game, falling to the floor and protecting the pieces of the painting with her own body.

Part 2, Section 12

Summary

Kambili continues to recover at Aunty Ifeoma's. Amaka tells her that Father Amadi was very worried about her—that Kambili is "Father Amadi's sweetheart." Amaka tells her cousin that Father Amadi's concern seems more personal, as a person might speak or be concerned about a sick wife. Kambili admits she has feelings for Father Amadi. Then Amaka asks if Kambili's father is the one who hurt her. Kambili admits that it was. That evening, Father Amadi stops by Aunty Ifeoma's to see how Kambili is doing. Kambili basks in the warm feelings she has in his presence as they make conversation and eat.

The next morning a woman from the university comes to the house to talk to Aunty Ifeoma. She tells Ifeoma that there is a list of lecturers who are "disloyal" to the university and that her name is on the list. Aunty Ifeoma rails against those who say speaking the truth is somehow disloyal. The woman asks her if the truth will feed her children. Later, Amaka explains that the sole administrator of the school was asking Ifeoma to "shut up." Obiora says he wishes that Ifeoma would get fired so they could move to America. Kambili, disturbed by the idea of Aunty Ifeoma's family moving to America, goes onto the verandah and watches Jaja work in Ifeoma's garden.

That evening Kambili watches Father Amadi coach young

athletes for a high-jump championship. On a water break, he comes to talk to Kambili. He touches her hair, and she feels a warmth spread through her.

The next day the university students riot, protesting against the sole administrator of the university, the head of state, and the lack of gas and electricity. The university closes down until further notice. Later that day four men in uniform come to search Ifeoma's house for documents "designed to sabotage the peace of the university."

Father Amadi comes to pick up Kambili the next day and take her to Mama Joe's stall at the market to have her hair braided. Mama Joe observes that Father Amadi looks at Kambili in a special way—that he is clearly in love with her. On the way back to Aunty Ifeoma's, they sing Igbo songs.

Analysis

Kambili has changed a great deal since her first visit to Aunty Ifeoma's house, as evidenced by her willingness to admit to Amaka both her feelings for Father Amadi and the fact of Papa's abuse. Some of this change, however, was already manifesting itself before Papa nearly kills her. In some ways she walks into the beating with her eyes wide open, as a result of the irrevocable changes wrought at Ifeoma's. However, her time in the hospital and the return to Ifeoma's home seem to have set these changes in stone.

Kambili's main worry now is losing what she has only recently gained. Aunty Ifeoma's moving to America seems to be an ever more likely outcome of the situation she is in. Father Amadi's vow of celibacy and future reassignment loom over their budding romance. Although their relationship seems destined to remain unconsummated, they do share moments of physical affection that are sweetly intimate. He touches her hair lovingly and takes her to have her hair braided. They sing together in the car. Father Amadi's influence on Kambili's life has been an overall positive one, helping to free her voice and experience a sense of love and joy that has been missing until now. Her physical attraction toward Father Amadi also signals Kambili's blossoming sexuality.

The university students' riot, Kambili and Jaja's rebellion, and Aunty Ifeoma's refusal to stop speaking the truth are all examples of a dynamic that pervades the novel. Tyrants try to rule with absolute authority and control, resorting to immoral behavior and corruption, and those who are oppressed defy them. The authorities then try to silence these voices of defiance. Sometimes there is a coup. Yet, as Papa has pointed out, sometimes a coup leads only to another coup. The unrest of this section suggests that the cycle of tyranny, rebellion, and violence is difficult to stop.

Part 2, Section 13

Summary

Kambili and Amaka go to church at St. Peter's, where Father Amadi celebrates the Mass. It is the kind of service Papa would not like, Kambili knows, but she enjoys receiving the Eucharist from Father Amadi. He drives Amaka and Kambili back to Ifeoma's house after Mass. On the way, he asks again about Amaka's confirmation name. She says she does not want to take an English name.

When they get back, Aunty Ifeoma is talking with her friend, Chiaku. Ifeoma tells Chiaku she has sent her CV (curriculum vitae, or academic résumé), to Phillipa, who now works at an American university. Chiaku criticizes this decision, saying that the "educated ones leave ... the weak behind. The tyrants continue to reign because the weak cannot resist." Obiora remarks that this statement is "unrealistic pep-rally nonsense." After Chiaku leaves, Ifeoma scolds Obiora for being disrespectful. Both Amaka and Kambili think about how Aunty Ifeoma's and Papa's discipline differs.

Unexpectedly, Mama arrives by taxi at Aunty Ifeoma's apartment. Mama is disheveled and wearing her slippers. Her eyes are "glazed over," and she says she isn't sure if her head is "correct." Papa broke a table over her belly, she tells them, and she miscarried a pregnancy once again. Mama cries until she falls asleep.

That night Papa calls and talks to Mama, who announces that she and her children will return home tomorrow. Aunty Ifeoma cannot understand why Mama is willing to go back with Papa. But Mama says Papa has been under a lot of pressure and cannot handle it alone. She says that Papa pays the school fees of a hundred people and saves lives. She also asks, "Where would I go?" Later, after Mama goes to bed, the cousins stay up playing cards. Amaka says Papa is not a bad man, he just doesn't handle stress well.

When Papa arrives, Kambili notices he is very thin and has a rash on his face. When they get home after the drive, Jaja observes that the purple hibiscus are about to bloom.

Analysis

The revelation that Mama has miscarried a second time implies her previous miscarriages were likely caused by Papa as well. This implication muddies the waters around the issue of Mama's inability to give Papa additional children. Mama mentions several times that his family and community encouraged him to take another wife or a mistress who could give him children and how grateful she is that he stayed with her. But now it seems as if Papa's beatings were responsible for her inability to carry a child to term. Mama's question "Where would I go?" seems more of an honest answer to the question of why she hasn't left Papa and perhaps the reason she goes back to him at this point. Of course, there's another reason, which will be revealed later.

The continuing question of whether Papa is a bad or good man is voiced for the first time by Amaka. She suggests that Papa is simply a man who does not react well to stress. This assessment may seem out of character for the progressive and principled Amaka, but it also may suggest the cultural pressure to excuse men's faults.

Details toward the end of the section foreshadow events that follow in Part 3, "The Pieces of Gods." Kambili notes Papa's rash in the opening section, and this, as well as his overall weakness, becomes a clue to the manner of his death. Jaja observes that the purple hibiscus flowers, which symbolize freedom and a new way of living, are about to bloom. This flowering symbolically leads into Jaja's new freedom from Papa's control, which will bloom in his act of rebellion at Palm Sunday Mass.

Part 3, Section 14

Summary

After Palm Sunday, the weather outside is stormy. Trees are uprooted, and satellite dishes have fallen off rooftops. Inside the house, silence descends. But it is as if the "old silence had broken and left us with the sharp pieces." Mama acts

differently. She doesn't whisper anymore or sneak food to the children. She has a hint of a smile, and Kambili notes "something hanging over all of us."

Jaja barricades himself in his room and refuses to come out to eat with the family even when Papa demands it and tries to push the door open. At dinner Papa eats little and drinks a lot of water. The rash on his face seems worse.

Yewande Coker comes to visit, bringing her daughter. She thanks Papa for helping send her daughter to a hospital abroad after Ade's death. Kambili goes to see Jaja, telling him about Yewande Coker's visit. Although the child is talking now, Jaja says, "she will never heal" from the trauma. As Kambili leaves the room, she pushes through the desk barrier Jaja has placed in front of his door. It moves easily. She wonders why Papa seemed to have trouble moving it.

On Good Friday Papa's hands are shaking badly, so the family decides to go to evening Mass. Aunty Ifeoma calls and tells Kambili that she is leaving to go to America and that Father Amadi has been called to Germany to do mission work. Then Jaja talks to Aunty Ifeoma. After the conversation, he tells Kambili, "We are going to Nsukka today. We will spend Easter in Nsukka." He informs Papa that he and Kambili are leaving. Although Kambili can't hear what Papa says, a few moments later Jaja says that Kevin will drive them. They leave.

At Nsukka, the talk is all about the upcoming move to America. The comfort and familiarity make Kambili feel the imminent loss of her aunt and cousins more deeply. Father Amadi arrives that evening. While he and Kambili talk in the garden, he stands close to her. Kambili expresses mixed feelings about going back to school and home. Father Amadi says he will try to get Father Benedict to recommend boarding school. That night, Kambili sings as she bathes.

Analysis

The opening lines of this section describe the stormy weather's destruction, as it uproots trees and dislodges the satellite dish. It also echoes the novel's opening line in which Kambili says things began to fall apart in her family on Palm Sunday. This section describes the aftermath of Jaja's rebellion and Papa's breaking the figurines. Things begin to fall apart on Palm Sunday, and they continue to fall apart quickly and with a vengeance. Kambili says that a new silence suddenly descends on the house, and then she likens the old silence to the figurines. Both the figurines and the old silence are broken and now have sharp edges that could cut them. As a symbol, the figurines represent the old silence—the way no one talked aloud about Papa's abuse but endured it secretly and silently. Both are broken now. But their destruction is not without consequences.

The idea of consequences is an important point because it would be easy to imagine that Jaja, having rebelled, is now free of Papa's tyranny and that perhaps Kambili soon will follow her brother's lead. And so they will live happily ever after. However, the old silence, when broken, can still harm them. There are ways that keeping silent for so long has damaged them and ways that speaking aloud about the years of pain and abuse will cause new and continuing suffering. Trauma, even when it is over, leaves scars. And sometimes the process of picking up the pieces of a life after a traumatic event can cause new hurts. This is the lesson Jaja tries to explain to Kambili when he says that Ade's child, who was psychologically traumatized by her father's death, will never fully heal.

The timing of the novel's events around Catholic holy days is a significant structural element of the novel, but in this section it seems especially significant. Palm Sunday marks the celebration of Christ as he triumphantly enters Jerusalem and is hailed as "he who comes in the name of the Lord." Good Friday marks Christ's crucifixion, and Easter is the celebration of his resurrection. On Good Friday, Kambili learns that both Father Amadi and Aunty Ifeoma are moving away, and these developments strike a staggering emotional blow. But Jaja and Kambili go to Nsukka for Easter, and though sadness is in the air, so is joy. For the first time, Kambili makes Amaka laugh. A cleansing rain falls, and then the sun comes out. As Kambili bathes, she sings.

Part 3, Section 15

Summary

Father Amadi stops by Aunty Ifeoma's to find out what name Amaka would like to take for her confirmation in the Church. Amaka tells him that she will not take an English name, insisting Igbo names can glorify God as well as English names. Ifeoma and Father Amadi both say she never has to use the

name again and that it doesn't really matter. But Amaka still refuses. As a result, she cannot take part in confirmation on Easter Sunday.

Aunty Ifeoma wants to go on the pilgrimage to Aokpe, especially because she will be moving away. Amaka and Kambili agree to go, but Jaja decides to stay at Ifeoma's home. Obiora says he will stay with Jaja. Father Amadi also decides to come along. Crowds of people are at the site; many shout ecstatically that they see Our Lady or fall to their knees in prayer. Kambili sees a vision of the Blessed Virgin in several places and senses a divine presence everywhere. On the way home, she says she saw and felt the Blessed Virgin, and Aunty Ifeoma agrees that "something from God" was going on at Aokpe.

Kambili accompanies Father Amadi as he says some of his goodbyes. In the car she declares her love for him, to which he responds, "You will find more love than you will need in a lifetime." The next day Aunty Ifeoma gets her visa to go to America. She begins making plans to move out of her apartment and buy the plane tickets. She talks about stopping in Enugu to see Papa and making sure Kambili and Jaja can go to a boarding school.

On Father Amadi's last day, Kambili is filled with anger at his leaving, but she promises to write to him in Germany. As they say goodbye, he holds her close. At dinner, she tries to lock away her feelings, but they emerge in a restless night of poor sleep and nightmares.

Taking a last tour of Nsukka before leaving, Jaja, Kambili, Aunt Ifeoma, and the cousins decide to climb a steep hill and survey the town. The climb becomes a race when Amaka takes off sprinting. Although she starts racing last, Kambili arrives at the top of the hill along with Amaka. Ifeoma says that she will need to find Kambili a trainer since she is such a good sprinter. Kambili laughs and thinks about how easy it is to laugh.

That evening Aunty Ifeoma receives a phone call. She screams, and everyone comes running. She hands the phone to Kambili, who hears her mother's voice: "Kambili, it's your father. They ... found him lying dead on his desk." Kambili has never considered the possibility that Papa could die, so his death seems impossible and unreal.

Analysis

This section starts with a few events that show where on the religious spectrum the characters are falling. Amaka is willing to go on the pilgrimage but unwilling to take an English name and so does not become confirmed. Catholics traditionally take on the name of a saint at confirmation, and Amaka's position on the name is ideological: she sees the taking of English names as a sign of colonialism, which she rejects. Yet, she accepts aspects of the Catholic faith that do not show such obvious signs. Father Amadi and Aunty Ifeoma are more tolerant of the colonial influence in their religion, just as they are more tolerant of Igbo traditions. Kambili seems to be following their example. She has visions of her own on the pilgrimage, showing her religious faith as now coming from within, not from Papa's influence. These visions are a sign of her maturing faith. She believes because of her own experiences, not because her father has told her what she must believe to avoid going to hell.

On the other hand Jaja seems to have decided he wants no part of his father's religion, so he stays home when the others go on the pilgrimage. Obiora also stays, but because he has been lukewarm toward Catholicism throughout the novel, his lack of participation is not unexpected.

After the pilgrimage, the real goodbyes begin. Aunty Ifeoma is able to secure her visa, and she and her children make their plans to go to America. Kambili admits her love for Father Amadi in a straightforward way, and Father Amadi finally says aloud what both of them must have known from the beginning. As Kambili notes, "Finality hung in the air, heavy and hollow." This detail shows the tie between the weather and the mood that has become so prominent as the novel has progressed. The air is heavy, just as the sense of finality feels almost suffocating to Kambili.

The race up the hill, and running in general, can be seen as a reflection of Kambili's progress in her journey to adulthood. She is no longer held back, as she once was, by fear and hesitance. As she told her school friend Ezinne, she likes running, and although it was an excuse at the time, it has proven true. She once ran out of fear. Then she ran to chase Father Amadi, who noted how her legs were good for running. Now, she runs to the top of the hill for the sake of fun and family togetherness.

Part 3, Section 16

Summary

Kambili and Jaja go back to Enugu. It is raining again. Mama methodically packs Papa's things and turns away all the visitors who want to mourn with her. Jaja feels he should have taken better care of Mama and pushes Kambili away emotionally. He scoffs at Kambili's ritualized response, "God works in mysterious ways," pointing out the stories of Job and Jesus. Kambili feels Papa's absence keenly and wishes she would hear his footsteps on the stairs, but Jaja and Mama both are emotionally unavailable.

Mama receives a phone call then informs Kambili and Jaja that the autopsy reveals Papa was poisoned. In a calm, slow voice, she tells them she started putting poison in his tea before she came to Nsukka. Thinking of the love sips, Kambili loudly asks Mama, "Why did you put it in his tea? ... Why in his tea?"

When the police arrive, Jaja tells them that he is the person who put rat poison in Papa's tea. They take him away.

Analysis

Kambili's fixation on the love sips demonstrates her emotional state. It is important to note that the next, final, section brings the story into the novel's present—thus, the events in the first section occur at a time when Kambili already knows her father's tea was the vehicle of his death. The memory of the love sips becomes even more fraught with emotion when she looks back on them as evidence that Papa loved her, even in his terrible way. In truth, however, Papa's ways of loving his children and wife are the reason Mama murders him. His love was always toxic, and Mama makes any love sips he might offer from his tea toxic as well.

Jaja has completely separated himself from Papa's legacy, rejecting not only his brand of Christianity but perhaps Christianity altogether. In noting that God treated both Job and Jesus badly, Jaja seems to question whether a God who allows Job to suffer and causes his own son to die is the kind of God he can worship. This sentiment is a marked difference from Kambili's, whose expression of Catholicism is more akin to that of Aunty Ifeoma's and Father Amadi's.

Jaja, who has claimed responsibility for many transgressions in order to protect his sister and mother, now claims that he is the one who poisoned his father. Readers may wonder if this act of protection will be enough to make Jaja feel as though he did enough to help Mama. He can never undo what was done to them, but perhaps his suffering can take the place of theirs.

Part 4, Section 17

Summary

It is three years later—the present of the novel. A new driver, Celestine, takes Mama and Kambili to the prison to visit Jaja. They've been there many times before over the past years. Mama has been different since Jaja went to prison. At first she claimed to have killed Papa, but no one believed her. Now, she's thin and broken. Many words remain unspoken between Mama and her children.

The head of state has died, and an interim government is in place. As a result of this change and the payment of many bribes, Jaja is set to be released from prison. Kambili and Mama will tell him the good news when they visit. Kambili reflects on the correspondence they've had from Aunty Ifeoma and Amaka, as well as the letters sent between herself and Father Amadi.

At the prison they tell Jaja he will be released soon. At first, Jaja doesn't seem to take it in. His eyes, Kambili says, are "full of guilt" because he doesn't think he did enough to protect her. There is silence as they sit together, but Kambili says, "it is a different kind of silence, one that lets me breathe." She wonders if they will ever be able to talk more about what has happened.

As Mama and Kambili leave the prison, Kambili makes plans for the future: to visit Nsukka and America, to plant more flowers, to plant orange trees. Above them, clouds are like dyed cotton wool, full of future rains.

Analysis

This final section is filled with poignancy as it relates the long-lasting legacy of the events that occurred three years earlier. Kambili and Mama have been on their own since Papa's death

and Jaja's imprisonment, and their lives are a routine of prison visits, letters from loved ones, and bribes paid at every level—they even bring food to the prison to bribe the guards. Just as the Igbo people have learned new ways of living in the aftermath of colonization, Kambili, Mama, and Jaja have found new ways of living and thriving in the wake of Papa's death.

The title of the section, "A Different Silence," sums up the message of this section. There are many things the family members still do not talk about and possibly never will. There are hurts that go so deep, they may be impossible to bring to light. Kambili admits that there are ways Jaja will not fully recover; he "will never understand that I do not think he should have done more." Mama is a shell of her former self, unable to function without help. For her part, Kambili keeps it a secret that she still offers Masses for Papa and wishes she could see him. She isn't sure Jaja will understand that her love for Papa persists despite all he did.

However, Kambili claims the silence now is different from the silence "of when Papa was alive." It lets her breathe. It lets her plan for the future. The final paragraphs of the novel describe planting flowers and visiting loved ones and favorite places. These are hopeful images. Ultimately, the new silence allows for hope, whereas the old silence did not, which is an improvement.

❝❞ Quotes

> *"Things started to fall apart at home when my brother, Jaja, did not go to communion."*

— Kambili, Part 1, Section 1

The opening line of the novel describes a turning point in the life of Kambili's family—after which Papa's tyrannical control over the family begins to weaken. Although resistance and rebellion may indicate positive changes—since Papa's behavior is so violent—they also introduce chaos into the well-ordered family. The opening line also refers to *Things Fall Apart* by Nigerian writer Chinua Achebe, a novel about the erosion of traditional culture as a result of colonial influences.

"I knew that when the tea burned my tongue, it burned Papa's love into me."

— Kambili, Part 1, Section 1

Before drinking his tea, Papa's custom is to offer Jaja and Kambili "love sips." Like Papa's brand of love, which is controlling and abusive, Papa's love sips cause pain and lasting damage. Kambili's experience of Papa's love is that it hurts. After Jaja refuses Communion, Papa is so angry that he does not offer the love sips. At the end of the novel, when it is revealed that Mama has been poisoning Papa in his tea, it becomes especially important that he did not offer the love sips on this occasion.

"We did that often, asking each other questions whose answers we already knew."

— Kambili, Part 2, Section 2

Kambili describes the communication between her and Jaja as consisting of nonverbal looks and gestures and, as here, words that take the place of real expression. Asking questions to which they already know the answers replaces deeper or more honest communication. Kambili goes on to suggest these questions and answers replace other questions they might ask, "the ones whose answers we did not want to know." Throughout the novel, what remains unsaid is just as important as, or more important than, what is said aloud.

"I did not even think to think what Mama needed to be forgiven for."

— Kambili, Part 2, Section 3

After Mama expresses a desire to sit in the car during the visit to Father Benedict's home because she has morning sickness,

Papa brutally beats her, and she miscarries the pregnancy. Afterward, Papa has the family say prayers for God to forgive Mama. Kambili joins in the prayers determined to get them right. Although most people would say Papa is at fault for his violence and more in need of forgiveness, Kambili doesn't question his placing the blame on Mama. This acceptance shows the hold Papa has on his family's thoughts.

"He was gracious, in the eager-to-please way that he always assumed with the ... white religious."

— Kambili, Part 2, Section 4

Papa's embrace of the culture and religion of white people shows the effects of colonialism. Though he is Igbo, he has embraced the colonial idea that white culture is superior. Throughout the novel, Papa shows this bias, often speaking English with a British accent when around white religious people, such as Father Benedict.

"I was not sure what my laughter sounded like."

— Kambili, Part 2, Section 6

Kambili dreams that she is laughing, and in the dream she feels the sound is not her own laughter. However, she recognizes that she laughs rarely, or not at all, so she wouldn't recognize the sound if she did hear it. Early in the novel Aunty Ifeoma's frequent laughter and Kambili's lack of it are important points of contrast. When Kambili learns to laugh, she shows the change that has resulted from Aunty Ifeoma's influence.

"You could say anything at any time to anyone."

— Kambili, Part 2, Section 8

Kambili's experience has been dominated by Papa's strict enforcement of rules and order. Everything in her life is policed by Papa, and many things remain unsaid for fear of his reactions. Conversation at meals is especially ritualized and controlled. In Aunty Ifeoma's household, the children speak their mind at all times, and the conversation at the table is raucous. Kambili feels it is completely uncontrolled, and it causes her deep discomfort at first.

"That's a hibiscus, isn't it, Aunty?"

— Jaja, Part 2, Section 8

Jaja is the first to notice the purple hibiscus growing in Aunty Ifeoma's garden. Typically, hibiscus flowers are red, but Ifeoma's friend, a botanist, created a version with a deep purple color. The flower becomes a symbol of freedom from, and even rebellion against, tradition, which Jaja embraces before Kambili does.

"Being defiant can be a good thing sometimes."

— Aunty Ifeoma, Part 2, Section 9

Aunty Ifeoma can see Jaja is beginning to open up to new ideas and subtly encourages him to push back against his father's oppressive rule.

"He was smiling ... He was smiling."

— Aunty Ifeoma, Part 2, Section 10

After Papa-Nnukwu dies, Aunty Ifeoma tells Kambili that even in death his face had a smile. Smiling and laughter are important in the novel, as Kambili seems unable to do either one. That he was smiling as he died suggests the joy present in Papa-Nnukwu—a joy Kambili lacks as the novel begins and learns as it progresses.

"The painting ... represented something lost, something I had never had, would never have."

— Kambili, Part 2, Section 11

Amaka makes a painting of Papa-Nnukwu and gives it secretly to Kambili, who hides it in her bedroom. When Papa finds out, he tears the painting to pieces and beats Kambili unconscious. To Kambili, the painting represents the family connections, especially with her grandfather, that she was denied by Papa's adversarial attitude toward Papa-Nnukwu's traditional Igbo practices.

"It was hard to turn my head, but I did it and looked away."

— Kambili, Part 2, Section 11

After Papa beats Kambili until she is nearly dead and must go to the hospital, he visits her there. Mama tells her, "Your father has been by your bedside every night these past three days. He has not slept a wink," praising Papa for being a good and loving father. But finally, Kambili has had enough. Though in terrible pain, she turns her head away at Mama's words. This is the first moment in which she seems to question her father's love.

"We did not scale the rod because we ... could, we scaled it because we were terrified ... we couldn't."

— Kambili, Part 2, Section 12

After watching Father Amadi coach local boys in the high jump, Kambili sees in this a metaphor for the difference between Aunty Ifeoma's parenting and Papa's parenting. Aunty Ifeoma sets the bar higher and higher, expecting her children to rise to the occasion and successfully get high enough to clear it. Papa sets a high bar as well, but he propels his children over it by fear, not by joyful expectation.

"The old silence had broken and left us with the sharp pieces."

— Kambili, Part 3, Section 14

After Jaja refuses to take Communion, defying Papa, and Papa breaks the figurines, the family is forever changed. This change is neither all bad nor all good. It marks the beginning of the end of Papa's oppressive rule. Mama speaks louder, smiles a little, and doesn't sneak around. Jaja continues to defy Papa without consequence. Yet, something about the new state of things is still going to hurt them, the way glass can cut after breaking. The symbol of the figurines as representing their submission to Papa's rule is clarified in this metaphor.

"Silence hangs over us, but ... a different kind of silence, one that lets me breathe."

— Kambili, Part 4, Section 17

After Papa's death, a kind of silence still exists, but it is not the fear-based, oppressive silence of constant worry about Papa's punishments. This change suggests that although not all the traumas of the past will be fully healed, their pain will lessen enough that breathing and even laughter become possible. The closing section of the novel is bittersweet as it describes the aftermath of Papa's murder, but it is also filled with the beginnings of hope.

🐦 Symbols

Figurines

The breaking of Mama's ceramic figurines of ballet dancers is mentioned in the first sentence of the novel. Later, Kambili reveals that Mama polishes them carefully each time Papa beats her. The figurines come to symbolize not only Papa's abuse but also the way this abuse is not openly acknowledged. As long as the figurines remain intact, Kambili, Mama, and Jaja endure Papa's violence by cleaning up, keeping quiet, and pretending nothing is wrong.

The smashing of the figurines marks a symbolic turning point. The family's silence about Papa's abuse, and their tolerance of it, is broken. Mama rejects the idea of replacing the figurines, noting they are no longer needed. She knows she has finished allowing Papa to beat her and the children—he will soon be dead by her hand. Jaja, too, has begun to resist Papa's authority—and in public. Significantly, Papa breaks the figurines with his own act of anger, suggesting his actions ultimately cause the uprising against him and his death.

Purple Hibiscus

In Aunty Ifeoma's garden, purple hibiscus flowers bloom. A departure from the typical red hibiscus, their color is the result of experimentation by Aunty Ifeoma's botanist friend Phillipa. Jaja becomes fascinated by the purple hibiscus, tending to them while he and Kambili stay with Aunty Ifeoma. When they go back home, Jaja secretly brings some of the purple hibiscus to plant in their own garden.

The experimental, rare color of the purple hibiscus symbolizes the freedom Kambili and Jaja begin to find when they are away from Papa's authority at Aunty Ifeoma's. The purple hibiscus expresses its beautiful and unusual color with confidence. After Jaja refuses to take Communion on Palm Sunday and Papa breaks the figurines, Kambili notes, "Jaja's defiance seemed ... like Aunty Ifeoma's experimental purple hibiscus: rare, fragrant with the undertones of freedom." Similarly, Kambili learns to speak up and express herself rather than do what Papa expects.

Love Sips

It's Papa's custom to offer "love sips" of his tea to his children, telling them that "you share[d] the little things you love[d] with the people you love[d]." Each time he drinks tea, he first invites them to take a love sip. Because these are the first sips of the tea, it is typically piping hot and burns Kambili's mouth. This ritual reassures her that Papa loves her. When "the tea burned my tongue, it burned Papa's love into me," she explains.

These love sips represent the relationship between Kambili and her father. She wants the love sip because she wants his love and wants to feel confident of it. But when she takes the love sip, or accepts the love of her father, she also gets hurt. From Papa's love sips, Kambili learns the lesson that love is painful and comes to believe the pain is actually a way of knowing she is loved. This practice is also reminiscent of the tradition of ancient (and some present) rulers who had tasters test food and drink to make sure it wasn't poisoned before they themselves would eat or drink. This suggests that Papa would sacrifice his children for his own safety and foreshadows Papa's ultimate poisoning.

Painting of Papa-Nnukwu

Kambili's cousin Amaka has painted a picture of Papa-Nnukwu, which Kambili admires though she also envies the close relationship Amaka has with Papa-Nnukwu. After Papa-Nnukwu dies and Papa comes to take Kambili and Jaja back home, Amaka secretly slips Kambili the painting. Knowing Papa will punish her for keeping a painting of a heathen, Kambili hides it. When she shows it to Jaja and Papa catches them looking at it, his punishment is fierce, almost costing Kambili her life.

For Kambili, the painting represents a relationship with her grandfather that she was never able to have. She longs for the connection with her extended family that she sees her cousins enjoying. She wishes she had been allowed to know Papa-Nnukwu before he died. The painting is a reminder of all she was denied, yet it is something—a small consolation for the loss of real connection. Ultimately, it is her longing for this

connection, more than the secrecy, that enrages Papa.

Walls and Fences

Walls and fences appear throughout the novel, as do other similar boundaries. For example, the compound in which Kambili lives is bounded by a high wall topped with electric wire. Aunty Ifeoma's garden is bounded by barbed wire. The prison compound where Jaja spends three years is surrounded by a tall wall. In Papa's schedules, segments of time are separated from one another by thick black lines.

These walls, fences, and other boundaries symbolize control and lack of freedom. Those inside the walls and fences often have limited access to the outer world. They also symbolize separation: Papa is concerned with separating his children from Igbo culture and anyone he sees as a negative influence. He separates their lives into chunks he can control. The fence around Aunty Ifeoma's garden is especially noteworthy, as it shows that sometimes a certain amount of freedom can exist within a situation that seems confining. In the end, it seems as though blooming despite limitations is, to some extent, a common human experience.

🎭 Themes

Public versus Private

From its very first pages *Purple Hibiscus* is a novel about living in two realities—the public and the private. By virtue of being a wealthy businessman and philanthropist, Papa is a minor celebrity in both Enugu, the city where he lives, and Abba, his hometown. At St. Agnes Church in Enugu, he is regularly used as an illustration of Christian behavior and piety in Father Benedict's sermons. In Abba, when he visits at Christmas, he is given respect equal to the traditional leaders and wealthy citizens. However, Papa's behavior at home paints a different picture. He is abusive, beating his children and wife for the slightest infraction. His violence is extreme and unreasonable.

He beats Mama frequently, causing miscarriages and hospitalizations. He deliberately disfigures Jaja's finger. He pours boiling water on Kambili's feet. He kicks her until she is unconsciousness.

The difference between Papa's public and private behavior is a source of internal conflict for his family. For example, Kambili is afraid of her father but at the same time proud of him and proud to be associated with him because of his reputation in the community. Furthermore, she wants him to be proud of her—not only because she is afraid of him but because on a deep level she believes he is right. If people at church and in the community believe he is a good man, then he must be a good man. If Papa says something is sinful, it must be sinful. It takes a long time for Kambili to begin to question her father's behavior.

The other way this theme plays out is by setting up a parallel between Papa's private behavior and the political situation. Papa is a tyrant in his home, whereas in public—through his newspaper—he is critical of the authoritarian government. When Jaja resists Papa's authority by refusing Communion, he has more in common with Papa's public persona than with his private one.

Religion as an Oppressive Colonizing Force

Religious faith and practice are a pervasive presence in *Purple Hibiscus*. The novel's time line is defined by religious holidays, and its settings include churches and pilgrimages. It is also the main source of tension between Papa and his father and sister. Both Papa and Aunty Ifeoma have converted to Catholicism, the religion of their colonizers, but their father, Papa-Nnukwu, has maintained his traditional Igbo beliefs and practices. Holding to an exclusive and rigid interpretation of Catholicism and terror of his and his family's damnation, Papa refuses to allow Papa-Nnukwu into his home and severely restricts his father's access to Kambili and Jaja. Similarly, Papa prefers that the Igbo language and songs be a minimal, if any, part of the mass. He disapproves of the blending of Igbo elements into the church service or daily prayers.

On the other hand, Aunty Ifeoma, also a practicing Catholic,

embraces a more inclusive practice of faith. She and her family say the rosary each night, as Papa does, but they intersperse the prayers with Christian praise songs translated into Igbo, reflecting a less fanatical hybrid adaptation to the presence and legacy of colonial forces. Furthermore, Ifeoma does not reject Papa-Nnukwu for his traditional beliefs and allows her children to take part in some Igbo rituals. She prefers to see similarities between the two religions, noting that Papa-Nnukwu's morning prayers are not so different from Catholic prayers. The two priests in the novel, Father Benedict and Father Amadi, also represent two ways of practicing Catholicism. Father Benedict is more of a purist, whereas Father Amadi integrates Igbo language into his religious practice and is tolerant of those who practice traditional religion, even as he teaches the Catholic faith.

Navigating this religious landscape is part of Kambili's character development. Brought up in Papa's strict and oppressive Catholicism, she is initially shocked by Aunty Ifeoma's practices. As she gets to know Aunty Ifeoma, Aunty Ifeoma's family, and Father Amadi, Kambili begins to accept their more tolerant version of Catholicism. Yet, it is not until Kambili goes on the pilgrimage and has a vision of the Virgin Mary that she seems to take ownership of her religious faith. This is a significant moment in her coming of age, as she moves from being a child who accepts the faith of adults to a person with agency in her own religious life.

Finally, religion provides a way to reconcile Papa's seemingly contradictory behavior. As tyrannical as Papa's behavior may be, it most certainly comes from his fear of sinning and going to hell. He is emotionally moved during the Mass; he is exuberant after the sacrament of confession, or reconciliation (penance); and he weeps over the perceived sins of his wife and children. However, instead of allowing the practice of confession to guide his family away from temptation and back into the favor of the Christian God, he demonstrates the violent and oppressive behaviors of his and his people's colonizers. Both Papa's life and death illustrate religion's power to motivate not only love but also fear and violence.

Silence and Voice

Life in Papa's household means keeping words under tight

control. Kambili either says what Papa wants to hear or remains silent. Whispering, surreptitious facial expressions, and small gestures make up the quiet language that Kambili and Jaja share and that Mama sometimes uses to comfort them after Papa becomes violent. This behavior replicates life under a tyrant who forbids free speech and punishes with violence anyone who dares speak out. This behavior is also a microcosm of the state of the country under the head of state. Those who speak out in criticism of the government—such as Aunty Ifeoma, Ade Coker, and even Papa—are often punished. However, even though he himself runs a newspaper that criticizes the tyrannical head of state, Papa does not seem to see the parallel in his own family.

When Kambili goes to stay with Aunty Ifeoma, both she and Jaja are far quieter than their aunt and cousins. Aunty Ifeoma's family laughs often and has nonstop lively, sometimes contentious, conversation. They are used to asking questions and challenging authorities. Kambili and Jaja's relative silence is so noticeable in contrast that Amaka, Ifeoma's daughter, wonders whether something is wrong with her cousins. Taking Kambili's silence as arrogance, Amaka accuses her of being a snob. As the visit continues, Jaja begins to open up and become more talkative, but at first Kambili has a hard time following his example. When she should speak, she coughs or stutters and can't get the words out. Over time, however, Kambili discovers her voice. She begins to talk more openly, to ask questions, and to sing along when her cousins or Father Amadi begin an Igbo song. She even begins to laugh.

The novel does not trace a simple journey from silence to freedom and expression, however. Though Kambili becomes more able to speak her thoughts aloud, even after Papa's death there are many things she does not say and many things she and Mama do not discuss. However, with Papa gone and Jaja about to be released from prison, the silence is somewhat different. They each carry a "new peace," although they do not talk about it. The old silence was imposed by fear, but the new one, for Kambili, is a kind of empowerment; she doesn't need to explain how she feels or what she does, she just feels and does. Kambili says this new silence is "one that lets [her] breathe."

Printed in Great Britain
by Amazon